# COUNTRY INNS
# COOKERY

COUNTRY INNS GUIDEBOOKS
FROM 101 PRODUCTIONS

COUNTRY INNS OF THE FAR WEST
Jacqueline Killeen, Charles C. Miller and Rachel Bard

COUNTRY INNS OF THE GREAT LAKES
Robert Morris

COUNTRY INNS OF THE OLD SOUTH
Robert Tolf

# COUNTRY INNS
# COOKERY

*Coralie Castle*
*Jacqueline Killeen*

*101 Productions*
*San Francisco*

COVER AND BOOK DESIGN BY PATRICIA GLOVER

Copyright © 1982    101 Productions

Printed and bound in the United States of America.
Distributed to the book trade in the United States
by Charles Scribner's Sons, New York, and in Canada
by John Wiley and Sons Canada Limited, Toronto.

Published by 101 Productions
834 Mission Street
San Francisco, CA 94103

1 3 5 7 9 11 15 17 19 KP 20 18 16 14 12 10 8 6 4 2

Library of Congress Catalog Card Number: 82-61102

ISBN 0-89286-202-5

# Contents

## ILLUSTRATIONS

COVER ILLUSTRATION: Magnolia Hotel, Yountville California. Line drawing by Roy Killeen. Color rendering by Patricia Glover.

The drawings of the Griswold Inn, the Homestead Inn, and Stonehenge were rendered by Roy Killeen especially for this book.

Drawings of the following inns are by Roy Killeen and have been reproduced from *Country Inns of the Far West,* copyright 1982 by 101 Productions: Heritage House, Little River Inn, Magnolia Hotel, Manka's/Inverness Lodge, Old Monterey Inn, Pelican Inn, San Ysidro Ranch, Sutter Creek Inn, Vineyard House, and Wolf Creek Tavern.

Drawings of the following inns are by Roy Killeen and have been reproduced with his permission from *Country Inns of the Great Lakes,* illustrations copyright 1982 by Roy Killeen: the Anderson House, the Dearborn Inn, Jamieson House, Schumacher's New Prague Hotel.

Drawings of the following inns are by Andra Rudolph and have been reproduced with her permission from *Country Inns of the Old South,* illustrations copyright 1978 by Andra Rudolph: Beaumont Inn, Chalet Suzanne, Cottage Plantation, Malaga Inn, River Forest Manor.

Drawings of the following inns were furnished by the inns and are reproduced with their permission; when ever the artist is known his or her name follows the name of the inn in parenthesis: Asa Ransom House (Judy Lenz); the Bird and Bottle Inn; the Buxton Inn (Virginia King); Colonial Inn; Columbia Gorge Hotel (Herbert E. Carlson); Dana Place Inn; the Golden Lamb Inn; Haag's Hotel; the Hope Houses (Steve Doty); the Inn at Sawmill Farm (Rodney Williams); the Lyme Inn; the Mainstay Inn (Betsey Bates and Tom Carroll); Old Lyme Inn (Gigi Horr-Liverant); the Red Fox Tavern (Ann Lackman); the Red Lion Inn (Doug McGregor); San Benito House (Pavesich); the Shelburne Inn (Noel Thomas); Union Hotel (Scott Gorsline); Wayside Inn.

# Introduction

America's best regional cooking is often found at country inns. Other American country inns offer exceptionally good European fare, often reflecting the ethnic heritage of the communities where the inns are located or sometimes the presence of a sophisticated chef who has fled the "big city" to find a more tranquil way of life.

In this book we have collected recipes from a representative group of country inns across the continent. In these pages you will find the traditional Yankee fare of New England, the down-home cooking of the Old South, recipes from the Pennsylvania Dutch and Shaker traditions, the ethnic potpourri that has become the California style, and the hearty rib-sticking dishes popular in the Middle West. You will also find some recipes that are classically French or German or Czech, brought to these inns by emigré chefs or their descendants. But isn't this "melting pot cuisine" part of the tradition of American regional cooking?

America's better country inns also pride themselves on using fresh produce and seafood, most often indigenous to the area; cooking their foods from scratch; baking their own breads and pastries; often putting up their own preserves and relishes—in many cases from fruits and vegetables harvested from their own gardens. Convenience foods you are unlikely to find. For after all, most of these innkeepers are dedicated to providing the traveler with a respite from the plasticized, computerized ways of commercial hotels and motels. They offer instead a sense of history, a return to the old-fashioned way of living—and cooking.

Our selection of inns for this book does not pretend to be comprehensive. In some cases we requested recipes from inns, but the chefs refused to divulge their secrets. In other cases recipes arrived too late to be included, or didn't arrive at all. And, of course, out there in this huge continent there must be some inns that we don't know about with extraordinary cooking.

We can guarantee, however, that all the dishes are delicious. All the recipes have been tested—often retested several times—in the home kitchen to make sure they work properly. In some cases the recipes have been modified for ease in preparation.

We hope you enjoy this armchair—oops, kitchen stool—journey to the country inns of America as much as we have enjoyed the research for this book, including the cooking, and, especially, devouring the results.

—Coralie Castle and Jacqueline Killeen

# NEW ENGLAND

*Connecticut, Massachusetts*
*New Hampshire & Vermont*

# Griswold Inn
*Essex, Connecticut*

The year 1776: The Declaration of Independence was signed. The *Oliver Cromwell*, first Connecticut warship of the Continental Navy, was launched in the shipbuilding town of Essex on the Connecticut River. And on that community's Main Street, Sala Griswold opened his new inn, the first three-story structure in the state. Other buildings were added later, and the inn's doors have remained open continuously under the ownership of only five families. The longest tenure—nearly a century—was held by the family of Thomas Ladd, who purchased the Griswold in 1883 to make it a "First Class Temperance Hotel." That mandate is no longer followed. The Griswold's Tap Room is a popular spot for potables dispensed from a Steamboat Gothic bar. During the reign of the Ladd family the inn changed from a stagecoach and steamboat stop to a relaxing hostelry for yachtsmen and vacationers. William G. Winterer, owner since 1972, continues the old-fashioned traditions of hospitality, especially in the dining room where the emphasis is on country fare and fresh foods. Some of the dishes even go back to the eighteenth century, like the following recipes of Mrs. Griswold.

## MRS. GRISWOLD'S GLAZED BRISKET OF CORNED BEEF

This unusual method of preparing corned beef results in a meat that is tender, juicy, succulent, and the color of rich burgundy. Cook more than you need; the leftovers make excellent sandwiches.

*Serves four to five*
One 2-1/2- to 3-pound brisket of corned beef
3 to 4 lemon slices
2 whole cloves
2 bay leaves, crumbled
Natural brown sugar

Place brisket in a deep glass or ceramic dish and cover with water. Add lemon slices, cloves, and bay leaves. Cover and refrigerate, turning occasionally, overnight or up to 36 hours. Preheat oven to 350°F. Remove brisket, pat dry, and trim neatly. Place in a flat roasting pan, fat side up, and cover entirely with a 1/2-inch-thick coat of natural brown sugar. Roast, basting frequently, 2-1/2 hours or until fork tender. Let sit at room temperature approximately 20 minutes before serving. Slice at table and serve with Mrs. Griswold's Red Cabbage.

## MRS. GRISWOLD'S RED CABBAGE

*Serves four to five*
1 medium head red cabbage, coarsely shredded (approximately 6 cups)
5 to 6 sour apples, unpeeled and thinly sliced (approximately 3 cups)
1/4 to 1/2 teaspoon ground cloves
6 tablespoons red wine vinegar, or to taste

In a large saucepan, combine all ingredients, stirring to mix well. Bring to a gentle boil and cook, tightly covered, 2 hours, stirring often. If cabbage and apples appear to be too dry, add water as needed during cooking period. Adjust with additional red wine vinegar to taste, reheat, and serve.

# The Homestead Inn
*Greenwich, Connecticut*

Built as a residence for a prosperous farmer in 1799, this lovely old building overlooking Long Island Sound later served as a boardinghouse, a private school, and, beginning in 1830, was operated as an inn. Successive modernizations and periods of neglect had taken their toll when Lessie Davison and her Greenwich neighbor, Nancy Smith, purchased the inn in the late 1970s. They vowed to make it one of the top hostelries in southern New England and commissioned the noted designer John F. Saladino to restore the property, which he did splendidly—to the tune of a million dollars. Next they hired French-born Jacques Thiebault, sous-chef at Manhattan's Le Cirque, to manage the kitchen. The inn's restaurant, named La Grange, is located in an eighteenth-century barn that at some unknown point in time was attached to the main building. The dining room spills out to wide verandas with views of the tree-covered acreage surrounding the place. Jacques' haute cuisine has won countless accolades for La Grange, along with a growing clientele from New York City—only forty-five minutes away.

## CASSOLETTE D'ESCARGOTS

*Serves four*

GARLIC BUTTER
4 tablespoons butter, softened
1 to 2 garlic cloves, smashed
2 teaspoons minced shallots
1 tablespoon chopped fresh parsley
Salt and freshly ground pepper to taste

24 snails
5 ounces chanterelle mushrooms*
2 teaspoons chopped shallots
1 tablespoon butter
1/2 cup heavy cream
1/2 teaspoon Pernod (optional)
Chopped fresh parsley

Mix all ingredients for garlic butter together well and set aside. Sauté snails, chanterelles, and shallots in 1 tablespoon butter 2 to 3 minutes until snails start to crinkle. Add garlic butter and let melt and swirl. Add cream and Pernod and cook, stirring frequently, until slightly reduced. Sprinkle with parsley and serve immediately.

*Available canned (Bona Vita from Poland). If unable to locate, use 1 to 1-1/2 ounces dried chanterelle mushrooms. Soak in hot water to soften, and drain before sautéing.

## ESCALOPE OF SALMON WITH SORREL SAUCE

*Serves four*

SORREL SAUCE
1/2 cup dry white wine
1/4 cup Fish Stock, page 113
1/3 cup dry white vermouth
2 large shallots, minced
6 ounces sorrel, tough stems removed, finely chopped
3 tablespoons butter
1 cup Crème Fraîche, page 131
Fresh lemon juice to taste
Salt and freshly ground white pepper to taste
Heavy cream if needed

2-1/2 to 3 pounds fresh salmon fillets or steaks
Butter and oil for sautéing
Fresh parsley sprigs

To make sauce, in a shallow saucepan combine wine, fish stock, vermouth, and shallots. Bring to a boil and reduce until almost evaporated. Add Crème Fraîche and, stirring almost constantly, reduce until slightly thickened. Sauté sorrel, covered, in 1 tablespoon of butter until soft. Add sorrel to sauce with lemon juice, salt, and pepper. Set sauce aside and keep warm. If holding and sauce becomes too thick, thin with a little heavy cream. Just before serving, swirl in remaining butter.

   Sauté salmon quickly on both sides in butter and oil. Do not overcook. Ladle sauce on 4 heated plates and place salmon on top. Make a narrow band of sauce on top of salmon and garnish with parsley.

## CORNISH HENS DIABLE
## THE HOMESTEAD INN

*Serves four*
4 Cornish game hens
1/2 teaspoon salt
1/4 teaspoon freshly ground pepper
1/2 cup safflower or corn oil
1 medium garlic clove, minced
1/4 teaspoon crumbled dried rosemary
1/4 teaspoon crumbled dried thyme
1/4 cup Dijon-style mustard
1 cup fine dry bread crumbs

Cut hens in half, remove backbones, wash, and pat dry. Sprinkle with salt and pepper and arrange in a shallow baking dish. Combine oil, garlic, rosemary, and thyme. Pour over hens, cover, and let marinate 30 minutes at room temperature or in refrigerator overnight. Preheat broiler. Place hens on broiler rack and brush with marinade. Broil 4 inches from heat for 20 minutes or until tender, turning several times and brushing with marinade. Remove hens and, with skin side up, spread with mustard and sprinkle with bread crumbs. Return to broiler rack and broil 2 minutes or until crumbs are golden brown.

# Old Lyme Inn
*Old Lyme, Connecticut*

Old Lyme is a picturesque village on the Long Island Sound. For one hundred years an Empire mansion, built on the town's main street in 1850, was the residence of the owners of a nearby three-hundred-acre farm. Then in 1950 the Connecticut Turnpike was built through the farmlands, and the mansion was converted into an Italian restaurant. When Diana Atwood bought the building in 1976, it was in deplorable condition, with the second floor burned out from a fire. But now she has fully restored the house, furnished it with antiques of the Empire period, and is operating an inn and French restaurant that regularly merits three stars in *New York Times* reviews.

## CREAM OF PUMPKIN SOUP

*Serves eight*
One 5-pound pumpkin
2 sprigs fresh thyme
1 leek, white part only, thinly sliced
2 celery stalks, thinly sliced
6 tablespoons butter
1/3 cup unbleached flour
1 quart chicken stock
1/2 teaspoon ground cinnamon
1 orange
12 parsley stems
2 bay leaves
3 cups heavy cream
Salt and freshly ground white pepper to
    taste
Roasted pumpkin seeds (optional)

Preheat oven to 350°F. Wash and halve pumpkin. Place a sprig of thyme inside each half, and place pumpkin cut side down on a baking sheet. Bake 1 hour or until pumpkin meat can be easily pierced with a fork. Cool and scoop out stringy pulp and seeds. Save seeds to wash and roast for garnish. Scoop out pumpkin meat and set aside.

Cook leek and celery, covered, in butter until softened. Sprinkle with flour, cook and stir several minutes, gradually add stock, and cook and stir until smooth and slightly thickened. Blend in pumpkin meat and cinnamon. Juice the orange, reserving orange shells, and add juice to soup. Tie orange shells, parsley, and bay leaves in a cheesecloth bag. Add to soup, cover, bring to a gentle boil, lower heat, and simmer 30 minutes. Discard bag and purée soup in a food processor or blender. Strain and return to clean kettle. Add cream and heat *just* to boiling. Season with salt and pepper and garnish with roasted pumpkin seeds.

## CHICKEN BRAISED IN APPLEJACK

*Serves eight*
4 large chicken breasts, halved, skinned, and boned
Seasoned flour
4 tablespoons butter
1/4 cup safflower or corn oil, or as needed
4 tablespoons minced shallots
1 cup applejack, heated
1 cup dry white wine
1-1/2 quarts heavy cream
2 tart apples
Salt and freshly ground white pepper

Dredge chicken breasts in seasoned flour. In a large Dutch oven or ovenproof skillet, heat butter and oil. A few at a time, brown breasts evenly on both sides. Remove breasts and set aside. Preheat oven to 350°F. Pour fat from pan and add shallots and applejack; flambé (see page 151). When flame has subsided stir in wine and cream. Cook, stirring often, until reduced by half. Return chicken breasts to pan, cover, and braise 20 minutes in oven.

Ten minutes before chicken is done, peel, core, and slice each apple into 16 wedges. Add to pan and return to oven. When chicken is tender, remove chicken and apples to a heated platter and keep warm. Further reduce sauce to desired consistency. Adjust seasonings with salt and pepper and pour sauce over chicken and apples.

## PEAR FRANGIPANE TARTE

*Makes one tarte*
One 9-inch prebaked pastry shell, page
    152

SYRUP
1-1/2 cups dry white wine
1-1/2 cups water
2 tablespoons fresh lemon juice
1 cup granulated sugar
1 cinnamon stick

7 to 8 pears

PASTRY CREAM
1/4 pound butter, softened
1 cup granulated sugar
2 eggs
1 teaspoon pure vanilla extract
3 tablespoons unbleached flour
1 cup toasted sliced almonds, ground

GLAZE
1 cup apricot jam
2 tablespoons kirsch, or to taste

Prepare pastry shell and set aside. In a deep skillet, combine syrup ingredients. Bring to a boil and stir to dissolve sugar. Working quickly, halve, core, and peel pears, dropping into syrup as you work so pears don't discolor. Cover and poach gently, turning several times, until just tender when pierced with a thin knife. Remove to a wire rack and drain well; cool.

While pears are poaching, preheat oven to 350°F and make pastry cream: Thoroughly cream butter and sugar. One at a time, beat in eggs. Stir in vanilla, flour, and almonds. Fill shell with mixture. Arrange pears cut side down on pastry cream. Bake 50 minutes or until pastry cream is golden; it will puff up over and around pears. Cool on a wire rack. When cool, prepare glaze: Heat jam, stirring, for 3 minutes. Add kirsch and cook and stir 1 minute. Cool slightly and spread over tarte.

# Stonehenge
*Ridgefield, Connecticut*

Ten acres of wooded Connecticut hills protect Stonehenge from the outside world. This vintage 1842 clapboard farmhouse with later additions nestles on the edge of a large lake inhabited by swans and flocks of geese. Stonehenge has been operated as an inn since 1947. But its food did not receive particular notice until the 1960s when two of New York's greatest restaurateurs purchased the place: Leon Lianides, owner of the Coach House in Greenwich Village, and Albert Stockli, who created many of the lavish dishes for Four Seasons and other establishments started by Restaurant Associates. Present owners David Davis and Douglas Seville, along with French chef Jean-Maurice Calmels, carry on the standards and traditions of Lianides and Stockli: live trout from the inn's pond, game in season, smoked sausages, pâtés and pastries made in house—all contributing to a string of *Holiday* awards since 1965.

# SAVORY PROFITEROLES

Make these *choux* in any size, tiny or large, to be eaten with a fork at table. Be sure to place them at least 1-1/2 inches apart on the cookie sheets, for they will double in size. Baking time will vary according to size.

*Makes about seven dozen*

CHOUX PASTE
1-1/4 cups light beer
1/4 pound butter, cut up
1/4 teaspoon salt, or to taste
1-1/4 cups unbleached flour
6 eggs

FILLING
3 tablespoons butter
3 tablespoons unbleached flour
2 cups milk
1/4 teaspoon salt
1/8 teaspoon freshly ground pepper
1/8 teaspoon grated nutmeg
Chopped fresh parsley or dill to taste
1 pound broken shrimp, miniature white
   shrimp, or bay shrimp

To make *choux*, over medium heat combine beer, butter, and salt. Bring to a boil, stirring to melt butter. Pour in flour all at once and stir rapidly until dough leaves sides of saucepan and forms a ball.

Remove from heat and let stand 15 minutes. One at a time, beat in eggs, making sure dough becomes smooth after each addition. Cover and refrigerate up to 3 days.

When ready to bake, preheat oven to 400°F. Place *choux* paste in a pastry bag and squeeze onto greased cookie sheets in walnut-sized mounds; bake 10 minutes. Reduce oven heat to 325°F. and continue baking 10 to 20 minutes. Remove from oven and quickly prick each *chou* several times with tines of a fork to release steam. Turn off oven heat and return *choux* to oven for 5 minutes. Cool on wire rack and store in a plastic bag, or freeze to be filled at a future time.

To make filling, in a heavy saucepan melt butter until bubbly. Stir in flour and cook and stir 3 minutes. Gradually add milk, stirring well so mixture doesn't lump. Add seasonings and parsley and cook, stirring often, 10 minutes. Remove from heat and cover with buttered waxed paper so skin doesn't form. When ready to fill *choux*, stir in shrimp and adjust seasonings to taste.

Preheat oven to 325°F. To fill, cut tiny tops off *choux* and pipe or spoon filling in. Replace tops and wrap loosely in foil, leaving top of foil open. Place on cookie sheets and bake 15 minutes or until filling is heated through and *choux* are lightly crisp. Serve immediately. If freezing filled *choux*, let thaw before baking.

# PHEASANT
## WITH CHAMPAGNE SAUERKRAUT
## AND GLAZED CHESTNUTS

*Serves four*
1 pound fresh sauerkraut
1 medium onion, minced
4 slices bacon, diced
2-1/2 cups champagne (leftover is all right because it loses its sparkle in cooking anyway)
Two 2-1/2- to 3-pound pheasants
1 teaspoon salt
1 teaspoon minced fresh sage, or
1/2 teaspoon crumbled dried sage
2 tablespoons butter, softened
1 tablespoon brandy
1 teaspoon grated raw potato
Glazed Chestnuts, following

Rinse sauerkraut in cold water and drain well. In a large skillet, cook onion and bacon until onion is soft and translucent. Pour sauerkraut over onion and bacon and add 2-1/4 cups of champagne. Cover and simmer 1 hour.

Preheat oven to 450°F. Sprinkle salt on pheasants, rub skin with sage and butter, and place in a shallow baking pan. Roast 20 minutes. Remove from oven, cool slightly and split. Place halves on sauerkraut, cover skillet, and simmer 20 minutes or until tender. Remove pheasants and keep warm. Stir reserved 1/4 cup champagne, brandy, and grated potato into sauerkraut. Simmer 3 minutes or until potato has thickened mixture. Mound on a heated serving platter or plates, place a pheasant half on each and garnish with reheated chestnuts.

GLAZED CHESTNUTS
1 pound fresh chestnuts, or
3/4 pound dried chestnuts
3/4 cup firmly packed brown sugar
3 cups pure maple syrup

If using fresh chestnuts, place 12 or so at a time in a saucepan, cover with water and boil until skins can be peeled off with a sharp knife. Be sure to peel them while they are still hot or the inner brown furlike skin, which must be removed, will not come off easily. If using dried chestnuts, place in a saucepan and cover with cold water. Bring to a boil and then reduce heat. Simmer 40 minutes or until tender. Time will vary with each batch of dried chestnuts. Drain.

Put prepared chestnuts in saucepan with sugar and maple syrup. Bring to a boil, stirring to dissolve sugar, and cook, stirring occasionally, to 220°F or soft-sugar stage. Set aside. Reheat just before serving as a garnish.

## PUMPKIN PIE

*Makes one large pie*
1 unbaked 10-inch pastry shell, page 152
4 eggs
2 cups pumpkin purée
3/4 cup brown sugar
1/4 cup granulated sugar
1 teaspoon ground ginger
1 to 2 teaspoons ground cinnamon
1/4 teaspoon grated nutmeg
1/4 teaspoon salt
1 tablespoon unbleached flour
1-1/2 cups heavy cream
1/4 cup brandy
Brandy Hard Sauce, following

Prepare pastry shell; refrigerate. Preheat oven to 350°F. In a large bowl, beat eggs lightly and blend in pumpkin purée.

Combine sugars, spices, salt, and flour. Stir into pumpkin mixture until well blended and add cream and brandy. Mix well and pour into pastry shell. Bake 1 hour and 10 minutes or until entire filling has puffed and cake tester inserted in center comes out clean. Transfer to a wire rack and cool. Decorate with hard sauce rosettes.

BRANDY HARD SAUCE
1/4 pound butter at room temperature
3/4 cup powdered sugar, or as needed
Brandy to taste

Cream butter and sugar to desired taste and consistency. Add brandy. Place in pastry bag and form rosettes on a waxed paper–lined shallow dish or plate. Refrigerate at least 4 hours.

# The Red Lion Inn
## *Stockbridge, Massachusetts*

In 1773 Silas Pepoon built a small tavern in the Berkshire hills to serve as a stop for stagecoaches on the route from Albany to Boston and Hartford. A year later, delegates from surrounding towns convened here for a "Stockbridge Tea Party" to protest the use of imports from England, little realizing that this humble inn would later host five American presidents. Grover Cleveland, William McKinley, Theodore Roosevelt, Calvin Coolidge, and Franklin D. Roosevelt all were guests at the Red Lion, as were Nathaniel Hawthorne and Henry Wadsworth Longfellow. For more than two centuries this inn has continuously offered hospitality to travelers, though under a succession of names and owners. Since 1900 it has been known as the Red Lion, and since 1968 it has been owned by Senator and Mrs. John H. Fitzpatrick. The original tavern building, which had been enlarged to accommodate over one hundred guests, burned down in 1896, but was rebuilt the following year and again expanded in the middle of this century. Still the aura of the 1700s remains, along with eighteenth-century furnishings, Colonial pewter, Staffordshire china, and traditional New England cooking.

## YANKEE POT ROAST look at computer file too

*lovely*

*Serves eight to ten*
One 5 to 6-pound bottom round of
    beef, trimmed
1/4 cup safflower or corn oil
1 cup diced onions
1 cup diced celery
1/2 cup diced carrots
1/3 to 1/2 cup unbleached flour
2-1/2 cups hot beef stock
One 14-1/2-ounce can tomatoes
1/2 bay leaf
1/8 teaspoon crumbled dried thyme
Salt and freshly ground black pepper
    to taste
Strips of fresh vegetables

In a Dutch oven or heavy pot brown beef well on all sides in oil; remove to a plate. Add onions, celery, and carrots to same pan, adding more oil if needed. Sauté over medium-low heat, stirring occasionally, 15 minutes. Preheat oven to 400°F. Sprinkle vegetables with flour, stir well, and cook 10 minutes, stirring often. Add oil if needed to absorb flour. Stir in stock and cook, stirring, until thickened. Drain tomatoes, reserving liquid; chop tomatoes and add to sauce with liquid, bay leaf, and thyme. Return meat to pot and turn to coat with sauce.

   Cover tightly and cook 2 to 2-1/2 hours or until meat is tender. Remove meat and keep warm. Strain sauce, if you like, and adjust seasonings with salt and pepper. Cut meat across grain and ladle sauce over. Garnish with strips of fresh vegetables.

## INDIAN PUDDING

*Serves eight to ten*
4 cups milk
4 tablespoons butter
1/2 cup yellow cornmeal
1/2 cup unsulphured molasses
1/4 cup granulated sugar
1 cup chopped apples
1/2 cup raisins
4-1/2 teaspoons ground cinnamon
1/2 tablespoon ground ginger
1/2 teaspoon salt
1 egg, lightly beaten
Vanilla ice cream or whipped cream

In a large, heavy saucepan, scald 2-1/2 cups of milk and butter. Combine 1/2 cup of remaining milk with cornmeal and add to scalded milk/butter mixture. Stirring slowly to prevent scorching, cook over medium heat 20 minutes. Preheat oven to 325°F. Stir in molasses, sugar, apples, raisins, spices, salt, and egg. Cook, stirring occasionally, 5 minutes. Pour into a well-buttered 11x8x2-inch baking dish. Pour remaining 1 cup milk over and bake 1-1/2 hours or until pudding is set and a knife inserted in center comes out clean. Serve warm with ice cream.

# Dana Place Inn
*Jackson, New Hampshire*

In the 1860s Ontwin Dana built a large Colonial house on his rocky farmland at the base of Mount Washington in New Hampshire's White Mountains. He and his wife planned to rent rooms to summer guests, but soon their inn also became a food and drink stopover for stage coaches en route to the mountain top. When the Danas retired in 1914, they sold the inn to a doctor from Massachusetts for use as a summer house. Then in the late 1930s, when skiing was becoming a popular sport in the area, Dana Place again became an inn for both summer and winter visitors. Extensively remodeled and expanded several times in recent decades, the inn now includes twenty units on eight acres surrounding the original farmhouse. One of the old Colonial rooms still serves as a dining room where Continental dinners are served at fireside. Two newer dining areas provide views of flower gardens and apple trees. Among the popular entrées is the following Chicken Gloria: chicken with apricot and brandy sauce. Innkeepers Betty and Malcolm Jennings recommend serving it with rice pilaf and a spinach salad dressed with honey and lime juice.

# CHICKEN GLORIA

*Serves six*

SAUCE
1 cup orange marmalade
3/4 cup burgundy wine
3/4 cup water
1/2 cup orange juice
One 8-ounce can apricot halves, drained
    and puréed
2 tablespoons red currant jelly
2 tablespoons brown sugar
2 tablespoons cornstarch, dissolved in
1/4 cup water

Six 8-ounce chicken breast halves,
    skinned, boned and lightly pounded
Seasoned unbleached flour
Safflower or corn oil for sautéing
1/4 cup dry sherry
1/4 cup brandy
Halved apricots
Chopped fresh parsley

To make sauce, in a heavy saucepan combine marmalade, wine, 3/4 cup water, orange juice, puréed apricots, jelly, and brown sugar. Simmer gently over low heat, stirring frequently until well blended. Slowly add cornstarch mixture and cook and stir until thickened.

While sauce is simmering, dredge chicken breasts lightly with seasoned flour. Sauté in oil until golden brown on both sides. Drain on paper toweling. Pour oil from skillet and wipe out. Return chicken to skillet, add sherry and brandy, and simmer 2 minutes. Stir in apricot sauce, spooning over breasts to coat lightly. Transfer to a heated platter and garnish with apricot halves. Sprinkle parsley over all.

# Lyme Inn
## Lyme, New Hampshire

Salmon Washburn, who listed his occupation as "gentleman," built himself a handsome four-story residence in 1809 facing the commons in the quiet New Hampshire town of Lyme. In 1820 Erastus Grant added a two-story wing and operated Grant's Hotel, with apartments and a dancing hall, until 1870. Then Ezra Alden, a descendant of John Alden, bought the place and ran it as the Alden Tavern until 1938. In 1948 the building was converted to the Lyme Inn and is presently owned by Fred and Judy Siemons. Lyme is only a short distance from Dartmouth College and is a stop on the Appalachian Trail, attracting hikers in the summer and skiers in wintertime. Throughout the year, the Siemons set an excellent table, open to the public for dinners that mix Continental cooking with traditional New England foods. Seafood, such as the following Beer Batter Shrimp, is also a specialty.

## STUFFED MUSHROOMS

*Serves four to six*
16 medium-sized or 8 large mushrooms
1 cup drained canned minced clams
4 tablespoons butter, melted
1 teaspoon salt
1/4 teaspoon freshly ground pepper
1-1/2 teaspoons minced onion
Fine dry bread crumbs
Paprika

Choose firm, fresh mushrooms 2 to 3 inches in diameter. Clean by brushing with a soft brush, remove stems, and arrange caps cup side up in a well-buttered shallow baking dish. Preheat oven to 400°F. Chop stems of mushrooms to make approximately 1-1/2 cups. Combine with clams, butter, salt, pepper, and onion. Mound into caps and sprinkle with bread crumbs and paprika. Bake 20 minutes or until mushrooms are tender and topping is browned.

## BEER BATTER SHRIMP

This light batter may also be used for vegetables such as Swiss chard stems. The consistency may be varied: the more flour the thicker and puffier the coating. Stored in an airtight container in the refrigerator, it will keep several days; stir well before using.

*Serves four to six*
2 eggs
1/4 cup milk
1 cup beer
Salt and freshly ground pepper to taste
1 cup unbleached flour, or as needed
About 2 dozen large shrimp (1-1/2 to
   2 pounds)
Peanut oil for deep-frying

In a bowl, beat eggs lightly and combine well with milk, beer, salt, and pepper. Gradually whisk in flour, blending until smooth and adding more flour if thicker coating is desired. Refrigerate several hours or overnight. Heat oil, at least 4 inches deep, to 375°F. Working with 4 to 5 shrimp at a time, and stirring batter often, dip each shrimp into batter and drop into hot oil. Fry until golden, turning once; do not overcook. Drain on paper toweling and keep warm in a moderate oven until all shrimp are cooked. Serve immediately.

# BRANDY ALEXANDER PIE

*Makes one pie*

### CHOCOLATE CRUMB CRUST
1-1/2 cups finely crushed chocolate wafer
   crumbs
6 tablespoons butter, melted

### FILLING
1 tablespoon (1 envelope) unflavored
   gelatin
1/2 cup cold water
2/3 cup granulated sugar
1/8 teaspoon salt
2 eggs, separated
1/4 cup cognac
1/4 cup crème de cacao
1-1/2 cups heavy cream

To make crust, mix crumbs and butter well and pat into a 9-inch pie plate, covering bottom and sides. Chill thoroughly, or bake in a 300°F oven 15 minutes. Cool.

To make filling, in a heavy saucepan or top of a double boiler, sprinkle gelatin over water and let soften. Add 1/3 cup of the sugar, salt and egg yolks. Blend well and cook, stirring almost constantly, over medium heat or simmering water until gelatin is dissolved and mixture thickens to consistency of lightly whipped cream. Remove from heat and stir in cognac and crème de cacao. Refrigerate until mixture starts to set; do not allow to get too stiff. Beat egg whites until stiff and gradually beat in remaining 1/3 cup sugar until peaks form and mixture is glossy. Fold into gelatin mixture. Whip 1 cup of the cream and fold in. Mound in prepared crust and chill. Just before serving, whip remaining cream and, using a pastry bag, decorate top of pie.

# The Inn at Sawmill Farm
*West Dover, Vermont*

In 1968 architect Rodney Williams and his wife Ione, an interior decorator, bought a two-hundred-year-old farm and transformed its buildings into a country inn of enormous charm and distinction. The rustic siding of the remodeled barn is hung with old-fashioned farming tools. The inn furnishings are a blend of Colonial, Chippendale and Victorian. The dining rooms are appointed with gleaming crystal and silver, and provide views of a pond, gardens, and apple orchards. The surrounding acreage is also the site of a sawmill, built in 1771, for which the inn is named. The miller, Francis Snow, took up farming in 1779 and constructed the buildings that now house the inn. After the Williamses took over the place, their son Brill graduated from college in engineering and began to study cooking in the inn's kitchen. He was originally trained by his mother and later studied with a French chef, ultimately developing a style that mixes Continental cuisine with American specialties like Maryland backfin crab.

## CRAB MEAT IMPERIAL

*Serves six to eight as a first course*
1 cup mayonnaise
2 tablespoons Dijon-style mustard
1/2 medium onion, grated
One 8-ounce can water chestnuts, minced
One 2-ounce jar pimientos, minced
3 celery stalks, minced
2 green bell peppers, minced
Juice of 1 lemon
1 teaspoon salt
3 dashes Tabasco sauce
3 dashes Worcestershire sauce
Cayenne pepper to taste
1 pound flaked crab meat or crab lumps
Lettuce leaves
Fine dry bread crumbs
Butter

In a large bowl, combine mayonnaise, mustard, and onion. Stir in water chestnuts, pimientos, celery, bell peppers, lemon juice, and seasonings. Mix well, toss in crab meat, and adjust seasonings to taste. To serve cold, place lettuce leaves in crystal bowls set in a bowl of ice. Mound crab mixture into lettuce cups. To serve hot, preheat oven to 350°F. Mound mixture into buttered *coquilles* or scallop shells. Sprinkle with bread crumbs and dot with butter. Bake 15 minutes or until bubbly.

## MEDALLIONS OF PORK

This unusual method of cooking pork is well worth the effort; the result is tender and flavorful. The canning may be done as much as one week ahead if kept refrigerated. A two-pound pork loin will yield enough medallions to fill a one-quart jar and will serve at least four. Sawmill Farms serves this dish with baked apples filled with brandied chestnuts.

Pork loin
Salt
Reserved fat
Unbleached flour
Brandy
Heavy cream
Coarsely ground or crushed walnuts

Ask butcher to debone a pork loin, saving tenderloin for future use and bones for soup stock. Cut loin section into 3/4- to 1-inch slices. In bottom of a 1 quart widemouthed canning jar, sprinkle 1/2 teaspoon salt. Layer pork slices into jar, being sure to leave air space. Place jar(s) on a rack in a canner with cold water up to bottom of lids. Bring to a boil and, keeping water at same level throughout cooking period, cook at a slow boil 3-1/2 hours. Remove from canner and let stand until cool. Refrigerate until ready to use.

To remove meat from jar, place jar in warm water to melt gelatinous stock resulting from canning. Carefully take slices out, reserving any fat that has risen to top. For each serving, brown 2 medallions in a teaspoon or so of fat on both sides. Remove and keep warm. Stir 1/2 teaspoon flour into skillet, stir and cook several minutes and blend in 1 tablespoon brandy. Bring to a boil, stirring constantly, and add 1/4 cup cream. Bring again to a boil, stirring, and blend in 1/4 cup walnuts. Heat and pour over medallions. Serve immediately.

31

# COCONUT CAKE

*Makes one large cake*

CAKE
1/2 pound butter at room temperature
2 cups granulated sugar
4 eggs, separated
1 teaspoon pure vanilla extract
3 cups cake flour
1 tablespoon baking powder
1 cup fresh coconut milk*

ICING
2 egg whites
1/4 teaspoon salt
1/4 cup superfine sugar
3/4 cup white corn syrup
1 teaspoon pure vanilla extract

1/2 cup heavy cream, whipped with
1 to 2 tablespoons powdered sugar
Grated fresh coconut, or
Lightly toasted dried flaked coconut

To make cake, butter and lightly flour three 8-inch cake pans. Preheat oven to 350°F. Cream butter, add sugar, and beat until fluffy. Beat egg yolks lightly and blend into butter mixture. Stir in vanilla. Sift flour and baking powder and stir in alternately with coconut milk. Beat egg whites until stiff but not dry. Gradually fold into batter and pour into prepared pans. Bake 30 minutes or until cake shrinks slightly from edges of pans and a cake tester inserted in center comes out clean. Remove to a wire rack, cool, and remove from pans. Let stand on a rack until ready to assemble.

To make icing, beat egg whites and salt until stiff but not dry. Gradually add sugar and beat until smooth and glossy. Slowly pour in syrup and beat until very stiff. Fold in vanilla.

To assemble, place one layer of cake on a serving plate and spread with half of sweetened whipped cream. Cover with second layer and spread with remaining whipped cream. Top with third layer and frost entire cake with icing. Grate coconut over and pat it gently into frosting.

*Fresh coconut milk will make a more delicious cake, but if it is not available, bring 1-2/3 cups milk and 1 cup grated dried unsweetened coconut to a boil. Cool and force through a sieve to measure 1 cup coconut milk.

# THE MID ATLANTIC

*New York & Pennsylvania*

# Asa Ransom House
*Clarence, New York*

In 1799 the Holland Land Company offered lots near Lake Erie to "any proper man who would build and operate a tavern upon it." Asa Ransom, a young silversmith, was the first to accept this offer and built himself a home and tavern of logs in the wilderness. Later he constructed a sawmill and in 1803 the first grist mill in Erie County. The ruins of this mill are on the property of the inn named after Asa Ransom—although his original tavern has long disappeared and no one is quite sure where it was located. The present inn was built as a residence in 1853 and converted to a tearoom, the Millroad House, in the mid-1950s. In 1975 Robert and Judy Lenz took over the property, added dining rooms built in nineteenth-century style, and rechristened the place Asa Ransom House. The country dinners reflect New York farmland cooking, with such dishes as fricassee chicken with biscuits, smoked corned beef with apple-raisin sauce, and the house specialty: Salmon Pond Pie.

## CHILLED CITRUS SOUP

*Serves six*
2 grapefruit
1 orange
1 lemon
1 lime
1 quart orange juice
1/4 cup granulated sugar
1/4 cup cornstarch
1/4 cup cold water
1 cup chilled half-and-half or heavy cream
Fruit sections or berries

Peel citrus fruits and cut into medium dice. In a large kettle, combine fruit with orange juice and sugar. Bring to a boil, stirring to dissolve sugar. Dissolve cornstarch in cold water and add. Cook, stirring, 5 minutes until slightly thickened. Cool and refrigerate until icy cold. Add cream and ladle into champagne glasses. Garnish with fruit sections or berries.

## SALMON POND PIE

Asa Ransom House uses local white Cheddar cheese in all their cooking to avoid artificial coloring. Use a similar cheese such as Coon, Herkimer, or Tillamook.

*Serves four generously, six for luncheon*
4 tablespoons butter
1/4 cup unbleached flour
One 1-pound can tomatoes, lightly broken
1/2 cup diced celery
1/2 cup diced onion
1/4 cup diced green bell pepper
1 cup diced green beans, lightly blanched
1 cup grated white Cheddar cheese
7 ounces cooked or drained canned salmon, flaked
1/2 teaspoon seasoned salt
1/2 teaspoon paprika
1/8 teaspoon freshly ground pepper
Salt to taste
3 or 4 hard-cooked eggs, sliced

CHEESE PASTRY
1 cup unbleached flour
1 tablespoon baking powder
1/2 teaspoon parsley flakes
1/2 teaspoon celery salt
3 tablespoons cold butter
1/4 cup grated white Cheddar cheese
1/3 cup cold half-and-half cream, or as needed

In a large skillet, melt 4 tablespoons butter. Stir in flour and cook, stirring, several minutes. Gradually add tomatoes; cook and stir until slightly thickened. Add vegetables and cheese. Stir to melt cheese and with a fork stir in salmon. Add seasonings and gently fold in hard-cooked eggs. Spoon into 4 or 6 individual casseroles. Preheat oven to 425°F.

To make Cheese Pastry, combine flour, baking powder, parsley flakes, and celery salt. Cut in butter until mixture is consistency of coarse cornmeal. Stir in cheese and add cream all at once. Stir gently with fork until dough clings together to form a ball. Do not overmix. Roll and press to 1/4-inch thickness and cut circles to fit casseroles. Top casseroles with pastry circles, pressing down on edges. Bake 15 to 20 minutes until nicely golden.

## STRAWBERRY RHUBARB PIE

*Makes one pie*
1 recipe pastry dough, page 152
2 to 2-1/2 pounds rhubarb
Two 12-ounce baskets strawberries
2-1/2 tablespoons granulated sugar
1/3 cup cornstarch
1/4 cup unbleached flour
1/4 teaspoon grated nutmeg
1/4 teaspoon ground cinnamon
1/8 teaspoon salt
1/4 cup honey

Mix pastry dough and refrigerate. Slice enough rhubarb to measure 5 cups; set aside. Slice enough strawberries to measure 3 cups; set aside. Preheat oven to 350°F. In a large bowl, combine sugar, cornstarch, flour, spices, and salt. Toss in fruit and coat well. Toss in honey and mix well with 2 forks or with fingers.

Roll half of pastry into a large circle and place in a 10-inch pie pan. Trim edges to overlap 1 inch. Mound fruit filling into pastry and top with second round of rolled pastry. Trim, then pinch bottom and top edges together and crimp. Make slits in top crust in a pattern. Decorate with small cut-outs from pastry scraps. Bake 50 to 55 minutes or until pie is golden. Remove to a wire rack and let cool slightly before serving. Good with ice cream.

## The Bird and Bottle Inn
*Garrison, New York*

Located on five acres directly across the Hudson River from West Point, this inn was built in 1761. Known as Warren's Tavern then, it was a resting place on the New York to Albany stage road. In the early nineteenth century the steamboat replaced the stage for intrastate travel, and the tavern was sold to Justin Nelson, a prosperous farmer whose descendants lived there until 1916. The next owner eventually abandoned the place, but it was later restored to its original eighteenth-century appearance and reopened as the Bird and Bottle Inn in 1940. The dining room offers a mix of French and American cooking that has earned the inn *Holiday* awards yearly since 1979.

### BIRD AND BOTTLE BLACK BEAN SOUP

*Serves eight to ten*
2 cups black beans
2-1/2 quarts cold water
1 cup chopped celery
2 cups chopped onions
4 tablespoons butter
4 teaspoons unbleached flour
1/4 cup chopped fresh parsley
Rind and bone from smoked ham (1-1/2 to 2 pounds)
2 medium leeks, white and a little green, thinly sliced (about 3/4 cup)
2 bay leaves
1/2 tablespoon salt
1/4 teaspoon freshly ground pepper
1/2 cup Madeira or dry sherry
Lemon slices
Chopped hard-cooked egg

Wash and pick through beans. Cover with boiling water and soak overnight. Drain and put in a large soup kettle. Add 2-1/2 quarts cold water, cover, bring to a gentle boil, lower heat, and cook 1-1/2 hours. In a skillet, slowly sauté celery and onion in butter. Blend in flour and parsley, cook and stir several minutes, and gradually add 2 cups of beans and their liquid. Return to soup kettle, stirring to mix. Add rind and bone, leeks, bay leaves, salt, and pepper. Cover and simmer 2-1/2 hours, stirring occasionally, or until beans are tender. Discard rind, bone, and bay leaves. Drain beans, reserving broth, and put through sieve or food mill. Return to broth, stir in Madeira, and reheat. Float a lemon slice on each serving and sprinkle with chopped hard-cooked egg.

## FILLET OF SOLE

*Serves six*
3/4 cup dry white wine
2 to 3 shallots, finely minced
Six 6-ounce fillets of sole
2 large ripe tomatoes, peeled, seeded, and minced
1 cup sliced fresh mushrooms
1-1/2 cups Fish Stock, page 113

SAUCE
2 egg yolks
1/4 pound butter, melted
4 tablespoons butter
2 tablespoons unbleached flour
1 cup whole milk, scalded
1/4 teaspoon freshly ground white pepper
Dash grated nutmeg
1 cup heavy cream, whipped

Preheat oven to 350°F. Place wine and shallots in a large ovenproof sauté pan. Cook over low heat until wine is reduced to 1 tablespoon. Arrange fish over shallots. Cover with tomatoes, mushrooms, and fish stock. Cover and bake 15 minutes or until fish flakes easily when lightly prodded with a fork. Remove from oven. Drain and reserve stock for another use.

While fish is baking, make sauce. In a medium-sized bowl, beat egg yolks until thickened. Gradually beat in melted butter; set aside. In a small saucepan, melt 4 tablespoons butter. Sprinkle with flour; cook and stir 2 minutes. Gradually add milk; stir and cook until smooth and thickened. Cool and whisk in egg mixture. Add pepper and nutmeg. Fold whipped cream into sauce. Spoon over fillets and broil until golden.

## APPLE-ALMOND TARTE

*Makes two tartes*
2 prebaked 10-inch pastry shells, page 152

TOPPING
3/4 cup sifted unbleached flour
3/4 cup granulated sugar
1/4 teaspoon ground cinnamon
1/4 pound butter, chilled and cut into bits
1 cup chopped blanched almonds

5 Golden Delicious apples
3 to 4 tablespoons butter

3/4 cup heavy cream, whipped and
    sweetened with
1/4 cup powdered sugar (optional)

Prepare pastry shells and set aside. Preheat oven to 375°F. Combine flour, sugar, and cinnamon. Cut in the 1/4 pound butter and toss in almonds; set aside. Peel, core, and slice apples and arrange in pie shells. Dot with 3 to 4 tablespoons butter and cover apples generously with topping mixture. Bake 30 to 40 minutes until topping is golden. Remove to wire rack. Serve with whipped cream, if you like.

## Coventry Forge Inn
*Coventryville, Pennsylvania*

In 1954, when Wallis Callahan started
serving classic French meals in a Colonial
house in rural Pennsylvania, the odds of
finding an appreciative clientele seemed
slim. Yet the culinary reputation of
Coventry Forge Inn grew and grew,
bringing awards, and diners from many
miles away. Finally Callahan opened a
guest house with five luxurious bedrooms
to accommodate those who came long
distances to savor his cooking—among
them scores of celebrities ranging from
Hermione Gringold to Luciano Pavarotti.
This is Coventry Forge's second incarnation
as an inn. Built in 1717 as a residence,
the house was converted in the 1750s to
a wagoners' tavern known as the Rising
Sun Inn, which dispensed hospitality to
travelers until 1850. Then it again became
a private residence until Wallis Callahan
took over and made Coventryville a
major spot on the East Coast's epicurean
map.

## CREME DE CRESSON

*Serves six*
4 tablespoons butter
1/3 to 1/2 cup unbleached flour
1 quart chicken or beef stock
2 cups half-and-half cream
2 bunches watercress, trimmed of tough
  stems
1 tablespoon butter, or as needed
Salt and freshly ground pepper to taste

In a large heavy saucepan, melt 4 tablespoons butter until bubbly. Stir in flour
and cook, stirring, very slowly 20 minutes.
Do not allow to brown. Gradually blend
in stock. Cook and stir until smooth and
thickened. Lower heat and cook, stirring
occasionally, 30 minutes. Blanch watercress, drain, and simmer, covered, in 1
tablespoon butter 10 minutes. Purée
watercress in a food processor or blender
and stir into soup. Reheat and season
with salt and pepper.

## TRUITE AU BLEU

This is served as a first course at Coventry Forge. It also makes a superb luncheon dish or main course. Live trout, if available, are preferable. Stun the trout, then clean it quickly. Try to avoid removing the film on the body of the trout. Poach immediately.

*Serves four*
3 cups water
3 tablespoons white vinegar
4 trout, approximately 8 ounces each
Beurre Blanc Sauce, following

In a shallow saucepan large enough to hold trout without overlapping, bring water and vinegar to a boil. Immerse trout, lower heat, and simmer 4 to 5 minutes. Drain immediately, halve lengthwise, remove bones, and serve with Beurre Blanc Sauce.

BEURRE BLANC SAUCE
1/4 cup white wine vinegar
1/4 cup dry white wine
1 tablespoon minced shallot
1/2 pound butter, chilled and cut into
   small bits

In top of a double boiler over direct heat, bring vinegar, wine, and shallot to a boil. Reduce until almost evaporated. Place over hot water and gradually beat in butter bits a few at a time, allowing them to melt before adding more. Serve over freshly poached trout.

## ESCALOPE DE VEAU A LA CREME

*Serves six*
18 veal scallops
Equal amounts butter and safflower or
   corn oil for sautéing
2 to 3 tablespoons brandy, heated
3 to 4 tablespoons Madeira
2 cups heavy cream
Salt and freshly ground pepper to taste

Remove membrane from scallops and flatten with a cleaver. In skillet, heat butter and oil. Adding more butter and oil as needed, sauté scallops on both sides, a few at a time, just until tender. Add brandy and flambé (see page 151). When flames have died down, transfer to a serving platter and keep warm. Add Madeira and cream to skillet. Stirring almost constantly, bring to a boil and reduce to consistency of softly whipped cream. Season with salt and pepper and pour over veal.

# Haag's Hotel
*Shartlesville, Pennsylvania*

Surrounded by lush farmlands at the foot of the Blue Mountains, the village of Shartlesville was founded in 1765. Many of the three hundred inhabitants are descendants of the original Pennsylvania Dutch settlers and still speak that dialect. In 1915 Jacob Haag opened a hotel here, which four generations of his family have subsequently operated, serving copious quantities of Pennsylvania Dutch cooking family style in the large dining rooms. Over twenty bowls and platters per meal are passed around containing roast chicken, beef and ham, vegetables from the hotel's adjoining 125-acre farm, preserves and relishes made in house, home-baked cookies and pies. Following are recipes for some typical accompaniments, along with the Pennsylvania Dutch classic, Shoo Fly Pie. No one knows for certain how this pie came to be named, but the most logical of the many explanations is that the molasses filling is very attractive to flies.

## PEPPER CABBAGE

This salad is just as good the next day.

*Serves ten to twelve*
1/2 cup cider vinegar
1/2 cup granulated sugar
1/2 cup water
1/2 teaspoon salt
1 medium green bell pepper, thinly sliced
1 medium head cabbage, finely shredded
3 celery stalks, thinly sliced on diagonal

In a large bowl, combine vinegar, sugar, water, and salt. Toss in vegetables and refrigerate at least 2 hours.

## PICCALILLI

*Makes approximately seven pints*
1 gallon thinly sliced cucumbers
   (approximately six 12-ounce cucumbers)
8 small onions, thinly sliced
1/2 cup salt
3-1/2 cups granulated sugar
3 cups cider vinegar
2 tablespoons mustard seed
1 tablespoon celery seed
1 tablespoon ground ginger
1/2 teaspoon freshly ground black pepper
1/2 teaspoon ground turmeric

Combine cucumbers, onions, and salt.
Let stand 3 hours, stirring occasionally.
Rinse with cold water and drain. In a
large saucepan, combine remaining ingredients. Bring to a boil, stirring to
dissolve sugar, and simmer 10 minutes.
Add cucumbers and onions, stir well, and
bring just to a boil. Pack into hot
sterilized jars and seal.

## SHOO FLY PIE

*Makes one pie*
1 unbaked 9-inch pastry shell, page 152
1/2 teaspoon baking soda
3/4 cup boiling water
1 cup unsulphured molasses
1-1/2 cups unbleached flour
1/2 cup firmly packed brown sugar
1/4 cup shortening or lard, chilled

Prepare pastry shell and set aside. Preheat
oven to 375°F. Dissolve soda in water
and blend in molasses. Combine flour
and sugar thoroughly and cut in shortening
until mixture is consistency of coarse
cornmeal. Pour molasses mixture into
pie shell. Evenly distribute flour mixture
over. Bake 35 minutes or until a cake
tester inserted in center comes out clean.
Remove to a wire rack and cool.

# THE SOUTH

*Alabama, Florida, Kentucky*
*North Carolina, Virginia*

# Malaga Inn
## Mobile, Alabama

In the mid-nineteenth century, "twin" houses with "right-hand, left-hand" floor plans were popular among the wealthy families of Mobile. In 1862 brothers-in-law and business partners William Frohlic-stein and Isaac Goldsmith built such a pair, with double cast-iron filigreed balconies across the front. In 1967 real estate broker Mayme Sinclair bought the fine old town houses and, in a lavish restoration project, converted them into an inn. Her impressive guest list spans the worlds of politics and show business to include Nelson Rockefeller, Ronald Reagan, Bob Hope, Art Linkletter, and Mike Douglas. The food here combines French and Southern fare, with emphasis on fresh seafood from the Gulf of Mexico.

## SEAFOOD GUMBO

*Serves ten to twelve*
One 28-ounce can tomatoes
One 16-ounce can tomato sauce
1-1/2 quarts water
2 onions, finely chopped
1 pound okra, thinly sliced
1-1/2 cups finely chopped celery
1 garlic clove, finely minced
2 teaspoons salt, or to taste
1 teaspoon freshly ground pepper
1 tablespoon Worcestershire sauce, or
   to taste
2 pounds raw shrimp, shelled and deveined
1 pint shucked oysters
Tabasco sauce to taste
Cooked white rice

In a large kettle, combine tomatoes, tomato sauce, water, vegetables, salt, pepper, and Worcestershire sauce. Cover, bring to a gentle boil, lower heat, and simmer 40 minutes. Bring to a rapid boil, add shrimp and oysters, lower heat, and cook 10 minutes. Add Tabasco and serve with rice.

## CRAB MEAT AU GRATIN

*Serves six to eight*
1/2 pound onions, sliced
3 celery stalks, sliced on diagonal
1/2 pound butter
1/4 cup unbleached flour
One 13-ounce can evaporated milk
One 5.33-ounce can evaporated milk
2 egg yolks
2 pounds fresh white crab meat
10 ounces mild Cheddar cheese, grated
  (about 2 cups)
Salt and freshly ground pepper to taste

Preheat oven to 350°F. Sauté onions and celery in butter until soft. Add flour and blend well. Cook and stir 2 minutes and gradually stir in milk. Cook and stir until smooth and thickened. Remove from heat and beat in yolks. Add crab, two thirds of the cheese, and salt and pepper to taste. Transfer to a large shallow baking dish or 6 to 8 individual casseroles. Sprinkle remaining cheese on top and bake 15 minutes or until heated through and bubbly.

## PECAN PIE

*Makes one pie*
1 unbaked 9-inch pastry shell, page 152
3 eggs
3/4 cup granulated sugar
1 cup dark corn syrup
4 teaspoons butter, softened
Pinch salt
1 teaspoon pure vanilla extract
1 cup broken pecans

Prepare pastry shell and set aside. Preheat oven to 400°F. Beat eggs thoroughly and mix in remaining ingredients, blending well. Pour into pastry shell and bake 10 minutes. Lower oven temperature to 300° to 325°F and bake 50 minutes or until filling no longer shakes and a cake tester inserted in center comes out clean. Cool on a wire rack.

# Chalet Suzanne
### Lake Wales, Florida

Located on a seventy-acre estate in central Florida, Chalet Suzanne is surrounded by palm-fringed lawns and lush orange groves. The inn was created by Bertha Hinshaw a half-century ago and is presently operated by her son Carl and his wife Vita. From the beginning the food has been the focal point here, with all the recipes created either by Bertha or Carl. He now supervises the kitchen, inspecting almost every dish before it enters the antique-filled dining room. This care has earned the Chalet's restaurant a reputation as one of the outstanding dining places in Florida and numerous awards, including *Holiday* magazine's and the coveted four stars from *Mobil Guide*. Dinners usually start with broiled grapefruit. The shrimp curry, according to the Hinshaws, even wins the approval of guests from India.

## BAKED GRAPEFRUIT

1/2 grapefruit per person
Melted butter
Granulated sugar mixed with
Ground cinnamon
Chicken livers dusted with flour, salt,
  and pepper and grilled

Cut fresh grapefruit in half. Cut out
center and cut around sections to loosen,
being careful not to pierce skin. Fill
center of each grapefruit half with melted
butter, sprinkle with sugar-cinnamon
mixture, and broil until slightly browned.
Garnish each half with a grilled chicken
liver and serve as a first course.

## LAKE SUZANNE PEPPER JELLY

This jelly is made from hot peppers that
grow in certain areas around Lake Suzanne.
It is heavenly with Brie cheese and
crackers or with any cheese or meat.

*Makes about four pints*
6-1/2 cups granulated sugar
1-1/2 cups cider vinegar
1-1/2 cups coarsely ground green and red
  bell peppers (approximately 2 peppers)
1/4 cup coarsely ground red, white, yellow,
  or green hot peppers (do not seed)
One 6-ounce bottle liquid pectin, or
2 packages (3 ounces each) Certo

In a large saucepan, combine sugar and
vinegar until sugar is dissolved. Stir in
peppers and bring to a rapid boil.
Stirring to prevent sticking, boil 3 minutes.
Add pectin and boil 1 minute. Remove
from heat and let stand 5 minutes. Ladle
into hot sterilized jars, filling to 1/8 inch
from top. Seal and let stand without
disturbing for 24 hours.

## BLUE CHEESE MOUSSE DEAN

This mousse is very rich as a first course. It can be served as part of a cocktail buffet for many more people.

*Serves eight to ten*
12 ounces blue cheese or Roquefort
   cheese
1-1/2 tablespoons (1-1/2 envelopes)
   unflavored gelatin
1/4 cup cold water
6 egg yolks
6 tablespoons heavy cream
1-1/2 cups heavy cream, whipped
3 egg whites, beaten stiff but not dry
2 tablespoons poppy seeds
Endive or watercress
Toast rounds and/or crackers

Force cheese through a 1/4-inch mesh strainer with the back of a wooden spoon; set aside. In a heatproof bowl, sprinkle gelatin over water to soften. Place bowl in hot water and stir gelatin to dissolve; set aside. In a heavy 2-quart saucepan, combine egg yolks and 6 tablespoons cream. Place over medium-low heat and cook without boiling, beating continuously with a wire whisk, until mixture is consistency of thick heavy cream. Stir in dissolved gelatin and sieved cheese, blending well. Let cool to room temperature but do not let mixture start to set. Fold in whipped cream, egg whites, and poppy seeds. Pour into an oiled 2-quart mold and chill at least 6 hours. Unmold on a serving platter and garnish with endive or watercress. Serve with toast rounds and/or crackers.

# CURRIED SHRIMP
# WITH ORANGE RICE

*Serves four to six*
1-1/2 quarts water
2 tablespoons salt
1/4 cup fresh lemon juice
1 pound raw shrimp, shelled and deveined
1/3 cup butter or margarine
3 tablespoons unbleached flour
1 to 2 tablespoons curry powder
1/2 teaspoon salt
1/4 teaspoon paprika
Dash grated nutmeg
2 cups half-and-half cream
1 tablespoon finely chopped candied
　　ginger
1 tablespoon fresh lemon juice
1 teaspoon dry sherry
1 teaspoon onion juice
Dash Worcestershire sauce
Salt to taste
Orange Rice, following
Condiments, following

Bring water to a boil; add 2 tablespoons salt and 1/4 cup lemon juice. Drop in shrimp, stir with a fork, bring back to a rapid boil, and cook 2 minutes or *just* until shrimp turn opaque. Do not over-cook. Drain immediately. Put in ice water; cover and refrigerate.

In a heavy saucepan or skillet, melt butter and blend in flour, curry powder, salt, paprika, and nutmeg. Cook and stir 3 minutes. Gradually add cream; cook and stir until smooth and thickened. Add ginger and seasonings, stir in shrimp, and reheat thoroughly. Serve with Orange Rice and condiments.

ORANGE RICE
1 cup raw long-grain rice
1/2 cup orange juice
1 tablespoon freshly grated orange rind

Cook rice according to favorite method or package directions. Do not overcook. Add orange juice and rind and reheat.

CONDIMENTS
Chutney
Chopped salted peanuts
Chopped fresh parsley
Crisp bacon bits
Flaked coconut, plain or toasted
Chopped orange rind
Sliced apples dipped in lemon juice

## MUSTARD-CARAWAY LOAF

*Makes one loaf*
3 cups unbleached flour
1/4 cup granulated sugar
2 tablespoons baking powder
1 tablespoon caraway seed
1 tablespoon mustard seed
1/2 tablespoon salt
3 eggs, lightly beaten
1-3/4 cups milk
1/4 cup safflower or corn oil

Preheat oven to 350°F. In a large bowl, combine dry ingredients. Lightly beat eggs, milk, and oil to blend. Add all at once to flour mixture, stirring only until dry ingredients are moistened. Do not overbeat. Pour into greased 8-1/2 x 4-1/2 x 2-1/2-inch loaf pan and bake 1 hour and 5 to 10 minutes, or until bread pulls away from sides of pan and a cake tester inserted in center comes out clean. Remove to a wire rack, let stand 15 minutes, turn out onto rack, turn right side up, and cool.

*Chalet Suzanne*

## GATEAU CHRISTINA

*Serves eight to ten*

MERINGUES
4 egg whites
1/8 teaspoon cream of tartar
1 to 1-1/2 cups granulated sugar
1/3 cup ground blanched almonds

CHOCOLATE FILLING
2 egg whites
1/2 cup granulated sugar
2 tablespoons sweetened cocoa
1/2 pound butter, softened
4 squares (4 ounces) semisweet chocolate,
   melted

To make meringues, preheat oven to 250°F. Cut 4 circles of parchment paper and generously oil them (see Baking Hints, page 153); arrange on a large cookie sheet. Whip egg whites with cream of tartar until stiff but not dry. Gradually beat in sugar until mixture is smooth and glossy. Gently fold in almonds, being careful not to overmix. Divide mixture among the parchment circles and spread evenly to make flat circles, using a spatula. Bake 20 to 30 minutes or until meringues are almost dry. Remove from oven and flip over onto well-oiled cookie sheet. Carefully peel off paper and bake another 5 to 10 minutes. Meringues should be just starting to change to a golden color. When dry, remove from oven, let cool 5 minutes, and carefully transfer to a wire rack.

To make filling, in top of a double boiler over hot, not boiling, water, beat egg whites until frothy. Gradually beat in remaining ingredients, whisking continuously. Beat until mixture is thick and creamy. Remove from heat and cool.

To assemble, reserve approximately 2/3 cup of filling. Place best meringue layer on a serving plate. Spread with a layer of filling. Top with a second meringue circle, pressing down lightly so layers fit together. Spread with a layer of filling and repeat with third meringue. Place fourth meringue on top and carefully spread reserved 2/3 cup filling over it, allowing filling to drip down sides. Cover with a dome of aluminum foil and refrigerate 24 hours. To serve, cut in wedges with a serrated knife.

# Boone Tavern Hotel
*Berea, Kentucky*

Berea College built the Boone Tavern in 1907 on its 120-acre campus in the Appalachian area primarily as a guest house for the college. The Georgian-style hotel's reputation for Southern hospitality has since attracted visitors from all parts of the country. This inn is operated through an unusual "labor and learning" program at Berea College, in which all students participate in a mandatory work program that gives them college credits as well as financial assistance. About 80 percent of the tavern staff is students, many of whom are majoring in hotel management. The tavern has also become renowned for its emphasis on regional cooking, earning it the *Holiday* award, among others. The spoon bread for which Boone Tavern is so famous lives up to its reputation in every way.

## BAKED STUFFED PORK CHOPS

*Serves four*
4 very large rib pork chops, 1 to 1-1/2 inches thick
3 tablespoons minced onion
3 tablespoons butter or margarine
1-1/4 cups dry bread cubes
3/4 cup drained canned whole-kernel corn
1/4 teaspoon salt
1/8 teaspoon freshly ground black pepper
1/8 teaspoon ground sage
1 tablespoon water
Unbleached white flour
Salt and freshly ground pepper to taste
1/2 cup stock or water

Trim most fat from chops; set fat and chops aside. Sauté onion in butter until tender and, using a fork, toss with bread cubes, corn, seasonings, and water. Cut a slit from bone side of chops almost to fat side, making a pocket. Stuff each pocket with one fourth of the stuffing. Preheat oven to 325°F. In a heavy skillet, fry out a little pork fat. Sprinkle chops lightly with flour and brown in hot fat, turning once. Transfer to a shallow casserole and sprinkle with salt and pepper. Pour stock or water into casserole, cover tightly, and bake 45 to 60 minutes. Remove lid and bake an additional 15 minutes to further brown chops.

## SOUTHERN SPOON BREAD

*Serves eight*
3 cups milk
1-1/4 cups white cornmeal
3 eggs, well beaten
2 tablespoons butter, melted
1-3/4 teaspoons baking powder
1 teaspoon salt

In a large heavy saucepan, bring milk to a rapid boil. Immediately turn heat to medium and gradually add cornmeal, stirring constantly until mixture is very thick. Remove from heat and cool. Mixture will be very stiff. Preheat oven to 375°F. Break cornmeal mixture up into bowl of an electric mixer and add remaining ingredients. Beat 15 minutes. Spoon into two 8-inch-square casseroles or baking pans and bake 30 minutes or until bread begins to pull away from sides of casseroles and to turn golden. Serve from casseroles by spoonfuls.

## KENTUCKY DERBY PIE

*Serves eight to ten*
One 9- or 10-inch unbaked pastry shell, page 152
1/4 pound margarine
1 cup white Karo syrup
1 cup granulated sugar
4 eggs, beaten
1/2 cup semisweet chocolate chips
1/2 cup chopped pecans
Bourbon Whip, following

Prepare pastry shell and set aside. Preheat oven to 350°F. Cream margarine and blend in syrup and sugar. Beat well and blend in eggs until well mixed. Fold in chips and pecans and pour into pie shell. Bake 1 hour or until knife inserted in center comes out clean. Remove to cooling rack and let cool to room temperature. Decorate with Bourbon Whip just before serving.

BOURBON WHIP
1 to 1-1/2 cups heavy cream
3 tablespoons powdered sugar, or to taste
1/2 tablespoon bourbon, or to taste

Whip cream and fold in sugar and bourbon, adjusting to taste.

# Colonial Inn
## Hillsborough, North Carolina

The historic town of Hillsborough was once the capital of North Carolina, and since 1759 many of its illustrious visitors have headquartered at the Colonial Inn. Lord Cornwallis was a guest in 1781, and it's said that he ordered his men to pave the muddy streets in front of the inn. Aaron Burr was another noted visitor. The inn's twelve guest rooms and four dining rooms are decorated in Colonial American style and the menu features traditional Southern cooking such as the following specialties.

## CORNWALLIS YAMS

*Serves eight*

4 medium-sized sweet potatoes or yams
   (approximately 2-1/2 pounds)
2 eggs, lightly beaten
1 cup milk
1/3 cup crushed pineapple
2/3 cup granulated sugar
1/4 teaspoon salt
1/4 teaspoon ground cinnamon
1/4 teaspoon grated nutmeg
6 tablespoons butter, cut up
1/3 cup flaked coconut

Wash potatoes, place in a saucepan, and add water to cover. Cover saucepan, bring water to boil, lower heat slightly, and boil gently until potatoes are tender. Preheat oven to 350°F. Combine eggs, milk, and pineapple. Combine sugar, salt, and spices. Drain potatoes and when cool enough to handle, peel and mash. Stir in butter until melted and blend in milk and sugar mixtures. Pour into a well-buttered 11x8x2-inch baking dish. Bake 45 minutes or until potatoes are set and pull slightly away from sides of pan. Remove from oven and sprinkle with coconut.

## COUNTRY HAM WITH RED-EYE GRAVY

*Serves six*

Six 1/4-inch-thick slices country
  ham or other well-smoked ham
  (approximately 7 ounces each)
4 tablespoons margarine, or
  as needed
1/4 cup firmly packed brown sugar
1/2 cup strong black coffee

In a heavy skillet, sauté ham in margarine until light brown, turning several times. Remove from skillet and keep warm. Stir brown sugar into skillet drippings and cook over low heat, stirring to melt sugar. Add coffee; cook and stir 5 minutes until mixture is a rich red-brown color. Pour over ham slices and serve with hot biscuits.

## APPLE COBBLER

*Makes one large cobbler*

PASTRY
4 cups unbleached flour
1 tablespoon baking powder
2 tablespoons granulated sugar
1 cup shortening or lard
1 egg, lightly beaten
1/2 cup water

5 pounds tart apples
4 cups granulated sugar
1/4 pound butter, cut into small bits
1/2 cup water
2 tablespoons grated nutmeg
1 tablespoon ground cinnamon

To make pastry, combine flour, baking powder, and sugar. Cut in shortening until mixture resembles coarse cornmeal. Beat egg and water slightly and mix into flour mixture, stirring with a fork just until dough forms a ball. Flatten slightly and wrap well in waxed paper. Refrigerate at least 1 hour.

On a large board, roll dough into a rectangle about 16x21 inches. Cut thin strips from edges to make a rectangle about 12x18 inches; refrigerate strips. Line a buttered 9x15x3-inch baking pan with dough rectangle, pressing dough gently into sides and fluting slightly. Refrigerate while preparing filling.

Preheat oven to 400°F. Peel, core, and slice apples into thin slices. In a large bowl, toss with sugar, butter, and water, mixing well. Sprinkle nutmeg and cinnamon evenly over bottom of crust. Mound apple mixture into crust and decorate with reserved pastry strips. Bake 1 hour or until crust is golden and apples are tender. Remove to a wire rack. Serve warm or at room temperature.

# River Forest Manor
*Belhaven, North Carolina*

Lumber and railroad tycoon John Aaron Wilkinson's dream mansion took five years to build. From 1899 to 1904 workmen toiled to create this showplace in the Classical Revival style so popular at the end of the Victorian era, with Italian craftsmen called in to carve the ornate ceilings and the intricate mantels for each of eleven fireplaces. Two baths were so big that they contained oversized tubs for two. In 1947 the residence was purchased for an inn by Axson Smith, whose hotel management experience included stints at Chicago's Drake Hotel and the Palmer House. Over the years his hospitality and his bountiful table attracted to the stately mansion such guests as James Cagney, Talullah Bankhead, Harvey Firestone, and Burl Ives. Smith's traditions of innkeeping are now carried on by his widow Melba and son Axson Jr. One of these is the gargantuan nightly smorgasbord of some seventy-five dishes: salads, relishes, vegetables, meat, seafood, biscuits, and desserts, with emphasis on Southern down-home cooking. Crab in several guises is featured, with good reason: The coastal town of Belhaven is the crab processing center of the state.

## PAMLICO CRAB MEAT CASSEROLE

*Serves eight*
1 cup chopped celery
1/2 cup chopped onion
1 cup mayonnaise
Juice of 1 lemon
1 cup whole milk
Dash Tabasco sauce
2 cups seasoned croûtons
1 pound flaked fresh crab meat
Salt and freshly ground pepper to taste
1/2 cup fine dry bread crumbs
1/2 cup grated sharp Cheddar cheese

Preheat oven to 350°F. Combine celery, onion, mayonnaise, lemon juice, milk, and Tabasco. Toss in croûtons and crab meat and season with salt and pepper. Transfer to shallow baking dish and sprinkle with bread crumbs. Top with cheese and bake 15 to 20 minutes until heated through and bubbly.

## ESCALLOPED TOMATOES

*Serves eight*
4 cups solid-packed whole tomatoes (two 28-ounce cans)
2 tablespoons granulated sugar
1/4 teaspoon salt
1/2 cup chopped onion, cooked until soft in 2 tablespoons butter
1-1/2 cups toasted bread cubes
1/2 cup dry bread crumbs
Butter

Preheat oven to 350°F. Combine tomatoes, sugar, salt, onion mixture, and bread cubes. Transfer to a shallow baking dish and sprinkle bread crumbs over. Dot with butter and bake 15 to 20 minutes or until heated through and bubbly.

## FLUFFY LEMON PIE

*Makes one pie*
One 9- or 10-inch baked pastry shell, page 152

FILLING
1-1/2 cups granulated sugar
1-1/2 cups water
5 tablespoons cornstarch
3 egg yolks
1/2 cup fresh lemon juice

MERINGUE TOPPING
3 egg whites
1/4 teaspoon cream of tartar
6 tablespoons granulated sugar

Prepare pastry shell and set aside. To make filling, in a heavy saucepan combine sugar, water, and cornstarch, stirring to dissolve. Beat egg yolks and stir into sugar mixture. Blend in lemon juice and cook and stir almost constantly over medium heat until thickened to consistency of whipped cream. Cool, stirring occasionally, and pour into prepared shell.

Preheat oven to 325°F. To make topping, beat egg whites and cream of tartar until stiff. Gradually beat in sugar until mixture is glossy and forms soft peaks. Carefully spread over filling and bake 20 to 30 minutes or until lightly golden. Cool on a wire rack.

# Red Fox Tavern
*Middleburg, Virginia*

Since its establishment circa 1728 as Chinn's Ordinary, this Colonial inn has been steeped in American history. Originally it was the midpoint stop for coaches and horsemen on the route from Alexandria to the frontier, a route through rolling countryside that was surveyed by George Washington as a youth. During the Civil War the tavern served as a hospital and as a meeting place for Confederate General Jeb Stuart and Colonel John Mosby and his Mounted Rangers. In more recent years, President John Kennedy held one of his press conferences here. The five dining rooms, each with an open hearth, are decorated in the style of the eighteenth century. The menu is Continental with a few Southern specialties.

## SEVEN ONION SOUP

*Serves four to five*
1 large yellow onion, thinly sliced
1 large white onion, thinly sliced
2 medium red onions, thinly sliced
4 medium leeks, white parts only, thinly
  sliced
1 head garlic, minced
9 medium shallots, minced
4 tablespoons butter
2 cups dry white wine
2 cups chicken stock
2 cups beef stock
1 teaspoon tiny fresh thyme leaves
Salt and freshly ground pepper to taste
Dried French bread strips
4 to 5 slices Swiss cheese
Freshly grated Parmesan cheese
1 bunch green onions, finely sliced

Very slowly, sauté onions, leeks, garlic,
and shallots in butter, stirring often,
until dark brown and carmelized. *Do not
burn.* Deglaze with wine and reduce by
two-thirds. Add stocks and thyme, bring
to a gentle boil, lower heat, cover, and
simmer 30 minutes. Preheat oven to
450°F. Adjust seasonings with salt and
pepper and transfer to a heatproof tureen
or 4 or 5 heatproof individual bowls.
Float 3 or 4 bread strips on top, place a
slice of cheese over, and sprinkle with
Parmesan. Bake 5 minutes or until
cheeses are bubbly. Sprinkle with scallions
and serve immediately.

## SHRIMP RAVIGOTTE

*Serves six as a first course*
1 pound small raw shrimp, peeled and
  deveined

MARINADE
4 tablespoons drained capers
Juice from 1 large lemon
1/4 cup tarragon vinegar
1 tablespoon chopped fresh parsley
1 tablespoon chopped fresh chervil
1 tablespoon chopped fresh tarragon
1 small onion, finely minced
1 cup safflower oil
Salt and freshly ground pepper to taste
Finely shredded lettuce
1 large ripe tomato, peeled, seeded and
  finely diced

Bring a large pot of salted water to boil and drop shrimp in, bringing back to a rapid boil and cooking very lightly—just until barely tender. Immediately drain shrimp and plunge into a large bowl of ice water to retard further cooking.

Combine marinade ingredients, beating lightly to mix well. Add shrimp and refrigerate overnight, stirring occasionally. Drain and serve on bed of finely shredded lettuce and garnish with diced tomato.

## ROAST DUCKLING SOMERSET WITH GINGER SAUCE

*Serves three to four*
One 4- to 5-pound duck
Salt and freshly ground white pepper
6 ounces ginger root, minced
2 carrots, cut in strips
2 celery stalks, cut in strips
1 onion, halved and sliced in strips
1 cup dry white wine
2 cups chicken stock
2 tablespoons Brown Roux, page 151
3 to 4 tablespoons honey

Preheat oven to 350°F. Cut off wings of duck at first joint and reserve for stockpot. Remove giblets, slice, and arrange in roasting pan. Discard excess leg fat from duck and prick duck all over with tines of a fork. Salt and pepper inside of duck, rub with all but 1 tablespoon of the minced ginger root, and stuff with carrots, celery, and onion to puff out breast. Truss duck and place on giblets in roasting pan. Roast for 1-1/2 to 2 hours; *do not allow to burn.* During roasting time, turn pan around at least once to assure even cooking.

When done, set duck to cool, pour off fat in roasting pan, and deglaze with wine. Transfer to saucepan. Split duck in half. Remove excess skin, breast bone, ribs, etc., leaving only wing, thigh, and leg bone intact. Place on a warm platter and set aside. Add stock, bones, vegetables and skin to wine in saucepan. Boil until reduced by two-thirds. Thicken with Brown Roux, stirring to blend, and simmer 30 minutes. Skim off fat that accumulates and strain sauce. Coat duck halves with honey and reserved minced ginger root. Reheat in a 350°F. oven 15 minutes or until crisp. Serve with sauce.

# Wayside Inn
*Middletown, Virginia*

Travelers through the Shenandoah Valley have been coming to this inn since 1797, when it was known as Wilkerson's Tavern—first by foot and horseback, then by stagecoach, and finally by automobile, causing the Wayside to claim it was "America's First Motor Inn." But the Wayside is unlike any modern motor inn; it exudes the charm of the past, especially since the 1960s when a Washington financier purchased the place and furnished it with hundreds of antiques from his private collection. The seven dining rooms offer a wide choice of ambience, from the stately President's Room to the informality of the former Slave Kitchen. And presidents have dined here, beginning with George Washington, as has John D. Rockefeller, Paul Newman, and a host of other luminaries, choosing from a menu that features the favorite dishes of early travelers.

PEANUT SOUP

*Serves six to eight*
3-1/2 cups rich chicken broth
1 celery stalk, cut up
1 medium carrot, cut up
1 small onion, cut up
1 cup creamy peanut butter
One 13-ounce can evaporated milk
Dash granulated sugar

In a large saucepan, combine broth and vegetables. Cover, bring to a boil, lower heat, and cook slowly 15 to 20 minutes until vegetables are tender. Strain and discard vegetables. In same saucepan, gradually stir hot broth into peanut butter. Mixture may look curdled but will smooth out. Add milk and sugar. Stir and heat without boiling.

## WAYSIDE INN'S
## RABBIT CASSEROLE

*Serves two to three*
One 3- to 3-1/2-pound rabbit
1/2 teaspoon salt
1/4 teaspoon freshly ground black pepper
1/8 teaspoon crumbled dried basil
1 whole onion, cut up
1 carrot, cut up
1 stalk celery with leaves, cut up
1 garlic clove, smashed
Unbleached flour
Egg Batter, following
Safflower oil and butter for sautéing
3 whole mushroom caps
1/2 tablespoon butter, or as needed
1/2 onion, sliced
1 to 1-1/2 cups cooked wild rice

In a large saucepan, combine rabbit, seasonings, carrot, celery, garlic, and water to cover. Cover, bring to a gentle boil, lower heat, and cook 30 minutes or until rabbit is tender. Cool and remove rabbit. Strain liquid and reserve for use as a stock. Debone rabbit and dip pieces, a few at a time, in flour and then in batter. Sauté in oil and butter until delicately browned on all sides.

In a separate skillet, sauté mushroom caps in butter until golden. Remove with a slotted spoon and keep warm. Adding additional butter if needed, sauté onion slices in same pan until golden. Place rabbit pieces on beds of wild rice in individual casseroles, cover with sautéed onions, and top each serving with a mushroom cap.

EGG BATTER
2 eggs
1-1/4 cups milk
Salt and freshly ground pepper to taste
1 cup unbleached flour, or as needed

In mixing bowl, combine eggs, milk, salt, and pepper. Gradually whisk in flour, blending until smooth and adding additional flour if thicker, fluffier batter is preferred. Cover and refrigerate 1 hour or up to 2 days. Stir well before using.

## OLD-FASHIONED YEAST BREAD

*Makes three loaves*
2 tablespoons (2 packages) active dry yeast
1/2 cup lukewarm water
1 egg, well beaten, at room temperature
1 cup milk
1/4 cup granulated sugar
2 tablespoons butter or margarine
1 tablespoon salt
5 to 6 cups unbleached flour
Melted butter or margarine

In a large mixing bowl, sprinkle yeast over water, stir, and let stand until bubbly. Stir in egg and let stand 10 minutes. Scald milk and stir in sugar, butter, and salt; cool to lukewarm and add to yeast mixture. Gradually stir in flour to form a soft dough that leaves sides of bowl. Turn out onto a lightly floured board and knead 5 minutes, adding additional flour as needed to prevent sticking, until smooth and elastic. Form into a ball, place in an oiled bowl, turn to coat all surfaces, cover with a tea towel, and let rise in a warm place 1-1/2 hours or until doubled in bulk.

Punch down, knead 1 minute, shape into a ball, place in oiled bowl, turn to coat all surfaces, cover with tea towel and let rise in a warm place 1 hour or until doubled in bulk.

Punch down and divide into 3 equal portions. Form each portion into a loaf shape and place in 3 oiled 7x3-1/2x2-inch loaf pans. Cover with a tea towel and let rise in a warm place 1 hour or until doubled in size. Ten minutes before baking, preheat oven to 325°F. Bake loaves 20 minutes or until they are lightly golden and sound hollow when tapped lightly with fingertips. Turn out onto a wire rack, turn right side up, and brush with melted butter. Cool.

## AMBROSIA PIE

*Makes one pie*
1 baked 9-inch pastry shell, page 152
2/3 cup granulated sugar
1/4 cup cornstarch
1/2 teaspoon salt
3 cups milk
4 egg yolks, well beaten
2 tablespoons butter, softened
4 teaspoons pure vanilla extract
1 cup flaked coconut
1 cup heavy cream
1/4 cup powdered sugar
1/4 cup flaked coconut, toasted
Mandarin orange sections

Prepare pastry shell and set aside on wire rack. In a large heavy saucepan, combine sugar, cornstarch, and salt, mixing well. Combine milk and yolks thoroughly and gradually stir into sugar mixture. Stirring almost constantly, cook over medium heat until smooth and thickened to consistency of softly whipped cream. Remove from heat and stir in butter, vanilla, and coconut. Cool and spoon into prepared pastry shell. Whip cream until slightly thickened, gradually add powdered sugar, and beat until fluffy. Spread over filling, sprinkle with toasted coconut, and garnish with orange sections.

# THE MIDWEST

*Michigan, Minnesota*
*Ohio & Wisconsin*

# The Dearborn Inn
*Dearborn, Michigan*

This gracious Georgian-style hostelry was probably the world's first airport hotel! In the 1920s Henry Ford developed a short-lived interest in aviation and built outside of Detroit the Ford Airport, which he used as the manufacturing facility for his fledgling Stout Airlines. Later, passenger service commenced at the airport, but the nearest hotels were in downtown Detroit. Ford commissioned the noted architect Albert Kahn to design a luxurious inn to accommodate air travelers. In 1931 the Dearborn Inn opened its doors across from the airport, which closed two years later. But the inn continued to flourish. Today it is surrounded by thirty-two acres of landscaped grounds, which also contain a small "village" of replicas of the homes of Barbara Fritchie, Patrick Henry, Edgar Allen Poe, Walt Whitman, and Oliver Wolcott. Hollywood personalities—including Lassie—figure prominently among the latter-day celebrities who have stayed at the inn. All profits from the inn accrue to help support Ford's famous Greenfield Village and Henry Ford Museum, both just seven hundred yards away.

## DEARBORN INN
## VEGETABLE BEEF SOUP

*Serves twelve*

2 pounds meaty beef soup bones
Vegetable trimmings such as carrot
  peelings, celery tops, onion skins,
  stems of herbs
1 or 2 garlic cloves, mashed
4 to 5 peppercorns, lightly crushed
4 quarts cold water
Salt and freshly ground pepper to taste
2 or 3 carrots, diced
1 rutabaga or turnip, diced
2 celery stalks, diced
1 onion, diced
1 leek, white part only, diced
1 or 2 potatoes, diced (optional)
Blanched pearl barley (optional)
Cabbage wedges (optional)

Place bones in a soup kettle, cover with
salted water, and bring to a rapid boil.
Drain, wash bones in cold water, and
wash kettle. Return bones to kettle and
add vegetable trimmings, garlic, peppercorns, and cold water. Cover, bring to a
boil, lower heat, and simmer, skimming
off any surface scum, for 2-1/2 to 3
hours.

   Strain and return to kettle. Reheat and
season with salt and pepper. Bring stock
to boil and add remaining ingredients in
order given, cooking carrots 10 minutes
before adding rutabaga. Do not let

vegetables overcook. Cabbage will take
only about 5 minutes, so adjust additions
accordingly. Potatoes should be barely
soft.

## VEAL CUTLETS TAVERN STYLE

*Serves six*

BATTER
1 egg, lightly beaten
2/3 cup milk
1 teaspoon chopped fresh chives
1/2 teaspoon seasoned salt
1/4 teaspoon ground white pepper
1/2 cup plus 2 tablespoons unbleached
  flour

12 veal cutlets (2 to 3 ounces each)
Unbleached flour for coating
Equal amounts butter and safflower or
  corn oil for sautéing

DILL PICKLE SAUCE
6 tablespoons pickle juice
1 cup evaporated milk
1 tablespoon butter
1-1/2 tablespoons unbleached flour
3 or 4 tiny dill pickles
1/2 teaspoon Maggi, or to taste

Cooked chopped spinach or Swiss chard

Combine batter ingredients until well
blended; cover and refrigerate 2 to 3

hours or overnight. Preheat oven to 325°F. Lightly pound cutlets until thin. Lightly coat cutlets with flour and dip a few at a time into batter; sauté quickly in hot butter and oil until browned on both sides. As they are browned, transfer cutlets to a buttered baking sheet. Cover lightly with foil. Place cutlets in oven for 15 to 20 minutes to finish cooking.

While cutlets are cooking, make sauce. Combine 6 tablespoons pickle juice with evaporated milk. In a heavy saucepan melt butter until bubbly and sprinkle with flour. Cook and stir 3 minutes and gradually add milk mixture, stirring constantly until smooth and thickened. Do not allow to boil. Cut 3 or 4 pickles into tiny julienne to measure approximately 3/4 cup. Stir into sauce and season with Maggi, adding more pickle julienne if desired. Set aside and keep warm.

To serve, arrange 2 cutlets on each of 6 plates on a bed of cooked chopped spinach or Swiss chard and ladle sauce over corners of each cutlet.

## BREAD AND BUTTER PUDDING

*Serves six to eight*
2 eggs, lightly beaten
3 to 4 tablespoons granulated sugar
1/2 teaspoon salt
1 teaspoon pure vanilla extract
1/4 teaspoon grated nutmeg
4 cups milk
2 cups fresh bread cubes
Strawberry Sauce, following

Preheat oven to 350°F. In a large bowl, combine eggs and sugar until well blended. Add salt, vanilla, nutmeg, and milk. Place bread cubes in a well-buttered shallow baking dish. Pour milk mixture over and set dish in a pan of hot water. Bake 30 minutes or until a knife inserted in center comes out clean. Serve warm with Strawberry Sauce.

STRAWBERRY SAUCE
3 cups water
1 cup granulated sugar
1 tablespoon fresh lemon juice
1 cinnamon stick
One 12-ounce basket fresh strawberries
Brandy to taste

In a heavy saucepan, bring water and sugar to a boil, stirring to dissolve sugar. Add lemon juice and cinnamon stick. Cook, stirring often, until syrup reaches 255°F on candy thermometer. Crush 4 or 5 strawberries and add; cook and stir 4 to 5 minutes. Slice remaining strawberries, add to syrup and stir in brandy. Remove from heat and serve warm.

# The Anderson House
*Wabasha, Minnesota*

Built in 1856 with a view of the Mississippi River, the Anderson House is Minnesota's oldest operating hotel. In 1901 Ida Hoffman Anderson bought the hotel and started winning accolades for her cooking skills, learned in the Pennsylvania Dutch community of Lancaster, Pennsylvania. Ownership was passed from generation to generation of Andersons until 1964 when the hotel was sold out of the family and allowed to deteriorate. Then in 1976 Ida's great-grandson John Hall, with several years of hotel management experience, bought the place and renovated all the rooms. He also reintroduced "Grandma's Cooking," specializing in her renowned Pennsylvania Dutch recipes. Today the hearty fare is welcomed by visitors to the inn, including those who come to ski during winter and to fish or hunt during the other seasons. Grandma's breads, all made on the premises, are especially noteworthy.

## BEER CHEESE SOUP

*Serves twelve*
1-1/2 quarts milk
2-1/2 pounds American cheese, finely diced
Two 12-ounce cans beer

In a heavy saucepan, heat milk. Add cheese and cook, stirring constantly, until cheese is melted. Add beer. Cook, stirring, until heated and thickened.

## ANDERSON HOUSE BEEF ROLLS WITH MUSHROOMS

*Serves six to eight*
8 large thin slices of beef top round (3 to 4 ounces each)
Salt and freshly ground pepper
Prepared mustard
8 thick slices bacon
6 ounces ground lean pork
6 ounces ground lean beef
2 large onions, diced
Safflower or corn oil for browning, as needed
1/2 pound fresh mushrooms, thickly sliced
2 tablespoons butter, or as needed
2 tablespoons White Roux, page 151, or as needed
Beef stock as needed
Sour cream
Minced chives

Pound beef slices until very thin. Sprinkle with salt and pepper and spread with mustard. Place a bacon strip on each slice. Combine ground pork and beef and spread over bacon. Spread ground meat mixture with mustard and sprinkle with salt and pepper. From narrow ends, roll tightly and tie with kitchen string. Preheat oven to 350°F. Sauté onions in oil until they start to turn golden, push onions aside, and, without allowing them to touch, brown beef rolls on all sides. Transfer to a shallow baking pan, distribute onions over, cover tightly, and bake 1 hour or until tender.

While rolls are cooking, sauté mushrooms in butter until lightly golden. Transfer beef rolls to a heated platter, strew mushrooms over, and keep warm. Pour off surface fat from beef juices and gradually stir in roux. Cook and stir until thickened. If more gravy is needed, add more roux and beef stock. Pour over beef rolls and serve with sour cream and chives.

## SOUR CREAM RAISIN PIE

*Makes one pie*
1 baked 9-inch pastry shell, page 152
1 cup raisins
2 tablespoons water
1 cup granulated sugar
3 egg yolks
2 teaspoons unbleached flour
1/2 teaspoon ground cinnamon
1 cup sour cream

Prepare pastry shell and set aside on a rack. In a heavy saucepan, boil raisins and water, allowing water to boil away completely. Remove from heat and stir in sugar, yolks, flour, cinnamon, and sour cream. Blend well and, stirring almost constantly, bring to a gentle boil. Cook and stir until thickened to consistency of softly whipped cream. Do not overcook; mixture will thicken as it cools. Remove from heat and, stirring occasionally, let cool slightly. Mound into prepared pastry shell. Serve at room temperature.

## LEMON BREAD

*Makes three miniature loaves*
3/4 cup shortening or lard
1-1/2 cups granulated sugar
3 eggs
3/4 cup buttermilk
1-1/2 tablespoons freshly grated lemon peel
2-1/4 cups unbleached flour
1/4 teaspoon baking soda
1/4 teaspoon salt
3/4 cup finely chopped walnuts, pecans, almonds or hazelnuts

FROSTING
3/4 cup powdered sugar
1 tablespoon fresh lemon juice, or as needed

Grease three 5-1/2x3x2-inch loaf pans and line with waxed paper. Preheat oven to 350°F. In a mixing bowl, cream shortening and gradually beat in granulated sugar. Beat until smooth. One at a time, add eggs and blend in. Add buttermilk and lemon peel. Combine flour, baking soda, and salt. Stir into wet ingredients just until dry ingredients are moistened. Do not overmix. Fold in nuts and spoon into prepared pans. Bake 45 minutes or until bread has pulled away from sides of pans and a cake tester inserted in center comes out clean. Cool on a wire rack 10 minutes.

While bread is cooling, mix powdered sugar and lemon juice until consistency of softly whipped cream. Turn bread out onto rack, turn right side up, and drizzle frosting over, allowing it to run down sides. Cool before slicing.

# Schumacher's New Prague Hotel
## New Prague, Minnesota

As the name implies, many of the early settlers around the Minnesota town of New Prague were from Czechoslovakia; other settlers came from Germany. The New Prague Hotel, built in 1898, is a testimony to this heritage. The hotel was purchased in 1974 by John and Nancy Schumacher and was decorated in the style of the inns of Austria and Bavaria. Schumacher, a former Marriot executive chef, designed the menu around a Czech theme, with breads and pastries baked by local women whose ancestors came from that country. The entrées also include a number of classic German dishes, with much emphasis on game. John Schumacher recommends serving the following creamed rabbit with a green salad and red cabbage.

## CREAMED RABBIT

*Serves three to four*
One 3-1/2- to 4-pound rabbit, cut into
  6 pieces
Unbleached flour
Lard for browning
1/4 cup dry sherry
1/4 cup dry white wine
2 tablespoons minced shallots
1/2 cup water
1-1/2 pints heavy cream
Salt and freshly ground white pepper
  to taste

Preheat oven to 350°F. Dredge rabbit pieces in flour and brown on all sides in hot lard. Place in a heavy casserole and add sherry, white wine, shallots, and water. Cover tightly and bake 1 hour. Pour in heavy cream and continue baking, covered, 20 to 30 minutes or until rabbit is very tender and sauce has thickened. Season to taste with salt and pepper.

## DUMPLINGS

*Makes ten large dumplings*
4 eggs
2 cups unbleached flour
1 tablespoon baking powder
1/4 teaspoon salt
2 cups mashed potatoes
2 tablespoons farina (non-instant cream
  of wheat), or as needed

Bring a very large kettle of salted water to boil. In a large bowl, beat eggs lightly. Combine flour, baking powder, and salt and blend into eggs with mashed potatoes. Add farina to make a workable dough. With lightly floured hands, form into 10 ovals approximately 3 ounces each. One at a time, drop into boiling water; do not overcrowd. Lower heat slightly, cover tightly, and boil 15 to 20 minutes or until a cake tester inserted in center comes out clean. Quickly remove with a slotted spoon and drain on a wire rack, piercing each dumpling to release steam. Serve immediately, or slice with thread or floss, then brown slices in butter.

## APPLE STRUDEL

*Makes one large strudel*

PASTRY
4 tablespoons butter
1/4 cup water
1 egg at room temperature
1 tablespoon granulated sugar
1/4 teaspoon salt
1 teaspoon pure vanilla extract
1-1/3 cups unbleached flour or as needed

FILLING
1/2 cup crushed cornflakes
3 tablespoons butter, melted
1/2 cup fine dry bread crumbs
3 tablespoons fresh lemon juice
2 cooking apples
1 cup raisins
2/3 cup granulated sugar
1 teaspoon ground cinnamon

About 1/2 pound butter
1 tablespoon heavy cream, combined with
2 teaspoons powdered sugar

To make pastry, melt butter, add water, and cool to lukewarm. In a mixing bowl, beat egg lightly and blend in sugar until mixture is lemon colored. Blend in salt, vanilla, and butter mixture. Gradually beat in 1 cup of flour. Mix well and beat in remaining flour to form a stiff dough. Turn out onto a lightly floured board and knead 8 minutes, adding additional flour only if needed to prevent sticking. During this time, throw dough hard onto board 10 or 12 times to help elasticity to form. Dough will be soft and pliable. Form into a ball, place in a lightly floured bowl, cover with a tea towel, and let rest in warm place at least 45 minutes.

To make filling, combine cornflakes and melted butter. Toss in bread crumbs and set aside. Measure lemon juice into mixing bowl. Core apples and chop finely, tossing into the lemon juice as you work. Measure raisins and set aside. Combine granulated sugar and cinnamon; set aside.

To fill, place a large pastry cloth on a work surface or table. When dough is ready, heavily flour cloth, especially middle section, rubbing it in well. Place ball of dough on center and flatten with palms of hands. Lightly flour the dough and with rolling pin roll into a rectangle approximately 1 foot by 9 inches. Dust hands with flour and slide them palms down under dough to the center. Roll hands into fists and, using the back of your hands, gradually stretch dough from center out on all sides until paper thin. If dough breaks in a few spots, don't worry. Resulting rectangle should be approximately 2 feet by 18 inches.

To fill, preheat oven to 350°F.. Melt 1/2 pound butter and keep barely warm. Let dough rest 5 minutes. Brush entire surface with melted butter. Sprinkle with cornflake–bread crumb mixture. Place apples in a row along one narrow edge, brush with melted butter, sprinkle with raisins and sugar-cinnamon mixture, and fold in sides of dough along entire rectangle. If any edges appear too thick, gently cut or tear them off. Brush folds with melted butter and drizzle more butter over filling. Carefully lift cloth under filling edge and start to roll into a jelly roll, brushing excess flour off with a delicate brush and brushing with melted butter (continue to use cloth to help support roll).

Place seam side down on a buttered baking sheet. Bake 45 minutes or until nicely golden, basting with melted butter several times. Remove to a wire rack and brush with cream and powdered sugar mixture. Let cool slightly and brush again. Serve slightly warm. Strudel will reheat loosely wrapped in foil but may dry out and crumble more easily.

# The Buxton Inn
*Granville, Ohio*

Both the Buxton Inn and the Golden Lamb (following) claim to be Ohio's oldest inn, though the Buxton, built in 1812, qualifies its claim to that of "the oldest continuously operated inn in its original building." The first innkeeper, a pioneer from Massachusetts, named the place simply "the Tavern." It also served as a stagecoach stop and as the town post office. A later owner, a Major Buxton, gave the tavern his own name in 1865, and for four decades offered genial hospitality to visitors. The present owners restored the building in 1972. Over the years the Buxton has hosted such disparate guests as Harriet Beecher Stowe, Van Johnson, Ignace Paderewski, and John Philip Sousa. Rumor has it that the inn has even housed a ghost.

## BUXTON BEAN SOUP

*Serves eight*
1 cup navy beans (small white beans)
2 quarts water
2 celery stalks, chopped
1 onion, sliced
1/2 pound ham, chopped
2 bay leaves
1 garlic clove, minced
Salt and freshly ground pepper to taste

Soak beans in water overnight. Transfer to a soup kettle and add celery, onion, ham, bay leaves, and garlic. Cover, bring to a gentle boil, lower heat, and cook slowly 2 hours or until beans are tender. Season to taste with salt and pepper.

## BUXTON SIZZLING FILLET

*For each serving*
Three 2-1/2-ounce slices choice tenderloin
   of beef
1 slice onion
2 slices green bell pepper
1 large mushroom cap

Preheat broiler. Place one slice of beef on broiling pan. Top with onion slice, a second slice of beef, bell pepper slices, third slice of beef, and mushroom. Broil 5 minutes or until cooked to taste.

## WALNUT FUDGECAKE

*Makes one cake*
1-1/4 cup (2-1/2 sticks) butter
5 ounces semisweet chocolate bits or
   squares  cut up
6 eggs, lightly beaten
2-1/2 cups granulated sugar
3 cups unbleached flour
1/2 cup chopped walnuts

Preheat oven to 350°F. Melt butter, turn heat off, and stir in chocolate to melt; cool slightly. In a large bowl combine eggs, sugar, and flour. Add butter-chocolate mixture and blend well. Pour into buttered and lightly floured 11x17x2-inch baking pan and sprinkle walnuts evenly over batter. Bake 20 minutes or until cake begins to pull away from sides of pan and cake tester inserted in center comes out clean. Remove to a wire rack and cool.

# The Golden Lamb
*Lebanon, Ohio*

Vying with the Buxton (preceding) as Ohio's oldest inn, the Golden Lamb has been operating since 1803, though not always in the same location. The present four-story brick building was constructed in 1815 and restored with nineteenth-century furnishings in 1936. The inn's roster of illustrious guests includes ten United States presidents, Mark Twain, and Charles Dickens. The latter supposedly complained about the "lack of spirits"; the hotel had a strict temperance policy in its early days. The cooking is hearty fare. Lamb, of course, is often featured, as are Shaker specialties emanating from the large Shaker colony near Lebanon.

## PEPPER POT SOUP

*Serves four*
3 to 4 slices bacon, diced
2 small onions, chopped
1/2 green bell pepper, chopped
1 tablespoon butter, or as needed
1 tablespoon unbleached flour
1 quart well-seasoned beef or veal stock
*Bouquet garni* of
   1 celery stalk
   1 whole clove
   1/2 bay leaf
   2 parsley sprigs
   1 sprig thyme
   3 peppercorns, lightly crushed
1 large potato, diced
2 ripe tomatoes, peeled and cut up
Salt and freshly ground pepper to taste

DROP DUMPLINGS
1/2 cup unbleached flour
Pinch salt
1 egg, lightly beaten
3 tablespoons milk

2 tablespoons chopped fresh parsley

Sauté bacon, onions, and green pepper in butter until lightly browned. Sprinkle with flour, cook and stir 3 minutes, and gradually stir in 1-1/2 cups of stock. Cook and stir until smooth and slightly thickened; add remaining stock, *bouquet garni* (see page 151), potato, and tomatoes. Cover, bring to a boil, lower heat, and simmer 1 hour.

To make dumplings, mix all ingredients together. Adjust soup seasoning and bring back to a rapid boil. Place a colander over soup pot and force dumplings through colander into soup with back of a spoon. Boil gently just until dumplings are cooked through; they will rise to top. Sprinkle with parsley.

## BRAISED GOLDEN LAMB SHANKS

*Serves four*

2 tablespoons bacon drippings or shortening, or as needed
4 lamb shanks, cracked (10 to 14 ounces each)
Salt and freshly ground pepper
1/2 pound whole baby carrots, trimmed and lightly scraped
1/2 pound pearl or small boiling onions, peeled
1/2 cup sliced celery
4 ounces fresh mushrooms, halved or quartered
1 large garlic clove, minced

1 quart well-seasoned lamb stock, beef stock, or beef bouillon
1/4 teaspoon ground pepper
1/4 to 1/2 teaspoon minced fresh rosemary
1/2 teaspoon minced fresh thyme
1 bay leaf
2 tablespoons tomato paste
Salt and freshly ground pepper to taste
Minced fresh parsley

Preheat oven to 350°F. In a Dutch oven, heat bacon drippings. Sprinkle shanks with salt and pepper and brown, a few at a time, on all sides. Remove and set aside. Add carrots, onions, and celery to pot and brown lightly. Remove and set aside. Add mushrooms to pot and brown. Remove with a slotted spoon and set aside. Discard any remaining drippings and return shanks to pot. Add garlic, stock, pepper, rosemary, thyme, bay leaf, and tomato paste. Stir well and bring to boil.

Cover tightly, place in oven and braise 1 hour, skimming off surface fat often. Add carrots, onions, and celery and braise 15 minutes or until vegetables are almost tender and lamb is starting to pull away from bones. Add mushrooms and cook 5 minutes. Adjust seasonings with salt and pepper, sprinkle with parsley, and serve with sautéed green beans.

## SHAKER SUGAR PIE

*Makes one pie*
1 unbaked 9-inch pastry shell, page 152
1 cup firmly packed brown sugar
1/3 cup unbleached flour
2 cups half-and-half cream
1 teaspoon pure vanilla extract
4 tablespoons butter
Freshly grated nutmeg

Prepare pastry shell and set aside. Preheat oven to 350°F. Mix sugar and flour thoroughly and place in pastry shell. Combine cream and vanilla and carefully pour over. Dot with butter and sprinkle with nutmeg to taste. Bake 50 to 60 minutes until lightly golden. Cream will still shake but will set up after pie cools. Remove to a wire rack and cool.

# Jamieson House
*Poynette, Wisconsin*

This spacious Victorian mansion was built in 1878 by banker-lumberman Hugh J. Jamieson, a Scotch emigré who became a prominent civic leader in Wisconsin. But when Jeffrey Smith bought the place for an inn in 1972, the old house was a veritable wreck, with pigeons its only occupants. Today, after an exhaustive renovation, the Jamieson House glows with the elegance of yesteryear. Eight bedrooms are handsomely appointed with antique furnishings and replicated wallpapers. Downstairs, polished dark woodwork gleams in the candlelit dining room, where five-course table d'hôte dinners are served at formally set tables with silver rings encasing the linen napkins. A typical meal might include the following dishes, plus an aperitif, an hors d'oeuvre, and fresh garden vegetables with the main course.

## ZUCCHINI SOUP

*Serves six to eight*
1 large onion, sliced
1 garlic clove, crushed
2 tablespoons butter
2 tablespoons safflower or corn oil
6 small zucchini, sliced
1 teaspoon crumbled dried basil
1/2 teaspoon crumbled dried oregano
1-1/2 quarts chicken stock
1 to 2 teaspoons fresh lemon juice
1 cup heavy cream
Salt and freshly ground white pepper to taste

In a saucepan, sauté onion and garlic in butter and oil 5 minutes without browning. Add zucchini and herbs and continue cooking over low heat 5 minutes. Add 2 cups of stock, cover, and let simmer 15 to 20 minutes. Purée in a food processor or blender and return to saucepan. Add remaining stock, lemon juice, and cream. Reheat without boiling and season with salt and pepper to taste.

NOTE: If using fresh herbs, finely mince them and triple the measurements; add after puréeing. This soup is also excellent served cold, in which case the herb measurements should be increased slightly.

## BLUE CHEESE SAUCE FOR STEAK

*Makes two cups*
3 cups good dry white wine
1 pint heavy cream
1/4 pound unsalted butter, at room
  temperature
1/4 pound blue cheese

In a large, deep skillet or saucepan, bring wine to a rapid boil. Let boil until reduced to 1/4 cup. Lower heat and stir in cream. Boil, being careful liquid doesn't boil over, until reduced by half (1 cup plus 2 tablespoons); stir often and scrape sides so mixture doesn't cling to sides. Mix butter and cheese in a food processor or blender. Stir into cream mixture until melted and bring to a boil. Cool, stirring often, and put in a jar. Cover and refrigerate. When ready to serve over steak, place needed amount in a bowl and set in a pan of barely lukewarm water, stirring until soft.

*Jamieson House*

84

## POMMES DAUPHINE

These delicious puffed potatoes do not lend themselves to keeping hot or to reheating. Plan a menu with no other last-minute items.

*Serves six to eight*
2 pounds Idaho potatoes
4 tablespoons butter
1 teaspoon salt
2 egg yolks

PATE A CHOUX
1 cup water
1/4 pound butter
1 cup unbleached flour
4 eggs
Safflower, peanut, or corn oil for deep-frying

Peel and quarter potatoes. Place in a medium saucepan and cover with water. Bring to a boil, cover, and cook until tender. Drain immediately (save water for yeast breads) and shake pan over low heat to be sure all moisture is evaporated. Mash with an electric mixer and blend in butter, salt, and egg yolks.

While potatoes are cooking, make Pâte à Choux. Heat water and butter, stirring to melt butter. Bring to a rapid boil and remove from heat. All at once, add flour and beat just until smooth and mixture begins to form a ball. One at a time, beating well until completely smooth after each addition, beat in eggs. Thoroughly combine with potato mixture, cover, and refrigerate until cool. Pâte à Choux may be kept several days. Fill a fryer or a deep, heavy saucepan with oil to at least 6 inches. Heat oil to 375°F. Just before ready to serve, using 2 spoons, drop batter into oil and fry 5 minutes or until brown on all sides. Do not crowd fryer. Drain on paper toweling and serve immediately.

# HAZELNUT APRICOT TORTE

*Makes one torte*

CAKE
8 eggs, separated
1 cup granulated sugar
1-3/4 cups hazelnuts, lightly ground
1 tablespoon baking powder

APRICOT FILLING
1 cup apricot jam
10 canned apricot halves, chopped
1/4 cup firmly packed brown sugar
1/4 cup apricot brandy
Dash grated nutmeg

WHIPPED CREAM TOPPING
1 cup heavy cream
2 tablespoons powdered sugar, or to taste
1 tablespoon crème de cassis, or to taste
2 tablespoons white crème de cacao, or
   to taste

To make cake, oil a jellyroll pan (see Baking Hints, page 153) or three 8-inch spring-form pans. Line with parchment paper and oil the paper. Set pan(s) aside. Preheat oven to 350°F. Beat egg yolks until light and lemon colored. Gradually beat in 1/2 cup of sugar and beat until mixture is thick and forms a ribbon when poured from a spoon. Combine nuts and baking powder and fold into yolk mixture. Beat egg whites until frothy and gradually beat in remaining sugar until mixture is glossy and forms soft peaks. Gently fold into nut mixture one third at a time.

Spread batter onto jellyroll pan up to 1/2 inch of edges, or spoon into pans, distributing evenly. Bake 30 to 40 minutes or until edges begin to deflate or pull away from sides of pan. Let cool on a wire rack and turn upside down onto a cloth or sheet of waxed paper sprinkled with powdered sugar to prevent sticking.

While cake cools, prepare filling: Combine jam, apricots, brown sugar, and brandy. Heat and stir until well blended and slightly thickened. Season with nutmeg and set aside to cool.

Whip cream for topping, adding sugar to taste. Fold in liqueurs. To assemble torte: Carefully peel parchment paper off cake. Spread cake with filling, then with a layer of topping. Roll, place on a serving plate and frost with topping. If baked in round pans, spread one layer with filling and topping, top with second layer, and frost with topping.

VARIATIONS: Substitute walnuts for hazelnuts and fill with raspberry filling; substitute pecans for hazelnuts and fill with strawberry filling.

# THE WEST

*Arizona & California*

# Garland's
# Oak Creek Lodge
*Sedona, Arizona*

This rustic lodge is located on the banks of Oak Creek, in a verdant canyon amid the beautiful Arizona mountains—not far from the Grand Canyon. The first settlers here planted fruit orchards around 1900; the Todd family built the lodge in the early 1930s around the original home-steader's cabin, now the kitchen. Since 1972 the Garland family has owned and operated the place. Susan Garland, who had studied at La Varenne in Paris, set up the menu to feature fresh foods in interesting combinations. Her brother Gary and his wife Mary, who now manage the lodge, have carried on this tradition. From the ranch's three hundred fruit trees come peaches, apples, pears, apricots, plums, and cherries; organically grown vegetables come from the lodge's gardens; the breakfast eggs are laid by the Garlands' chickens; and even the trout served at dinner is caught in Oak Creek. Following is a typical dinner menu.

DALLAS SALAD

*Serves six to eight*

DRESSING
1/4 cup red wine vinegar
1 egg yolk
1/2 tablespoon minced fresh parsley
1 teaspoon minced onion
1 small garlic clove, minced
1 small shallot, minced
1 teaspoon Dijon-style mustard
1/4 to 1/2 teaspoon crumbled dried
   tarragon
3/4 cup plus 2 tablespoons olive oil
Salt to taste

One 16-ounce can hearts of palm*,
   drained and sliced
One 12-ounce can artichoke hearts,
   drained and quartered
3 avocados, cut into chunks
2 celery stalks, sliced on diagonal
Lettuce leaves

Blend all dressing ingredients except oil and salt in a food processor or blender. With motor running, gradually pour in oil until smooth and thickened. Taste for salt. In a salad bowl, gently toss vegetables, pour dressing over, and toss again. Serve on lettuce leaves.

*Do not substitute frozen hearts of palm.

## CORN CHOWDER

*Serves eight*
5 large ears of corn
1 quart chicken stock
Pinch granulated sugar
3 to 4 cups fresh corn kernels
3/4 cup chopped onion
1/2 cup chopped white of leek
1/2 cup chopped celery
1/2 cup chopped green bell pepper
2 tablespoons bacon drippings
1-1/2 cups diced peeled potatoes
1/4 teaspoon freshly ground pepper
1-1/2 cups half-and-half cream
Dash Worcestershire sauce
Dash Tabasco sauce
1 teaspoon crumbled dried oregano
Salt to taste
2 tablespoons minced parsley
Crisply fried bacon bits (optional)

Cut kernels from ears of corn, reserving both kernels and cobs. In a large kettle, combine stock, sugar, and corn cobs. Bring to a boil, lower heat, cover, and simmer 1 hour. Discard cobs. Measure 3 to 4 cups reserved corn kernels and sauté with onion, leek, celery, and bell pepper in bacon drippings until onion is softened. Add mixture to kettle and bring to a boil. Add potatoes and ground pepper, bring back to a boil, lower heat, cover, and simmer until potatoes are just tender.

Add cream, Worcestershire sauce, Tabasco, oregano, and salt. Simmer gently to reheat. Stir in parsley and garnish with bacon bits, if you like.

## CHICKEN OR VEAL WITH MOREL SAUCE

The morels in this recipe are available in seven-ounce jars, but they are difficult to find. Dried and soaked morels or fresh mushrooms may be substituted, but the flavor will be slightly different.

*Makes about two cups*

MOREL SAUCE
4 to 5 drained canned morel mushrooms,
    2 ounces fresh mushrooms, or
    1 ounce dried morel mushrooms
3 tablespoons rendered chicken fat
1 tablespoon unbleached flour
1/2 cup dry white wine
1-1/2 cups chicken stock
1 cup heavy cream
Salt and freshly ground white pepper
    to taste

6 chicken breasts, halved, boned, and
    skinned, or
24 thinly sliced veal scallops
Seasoned flour
Butter and safflower or corn oil for
    sautéing

Finely mince canned mushrooms and sauté in fat until they begin to pop. If using fresh mushrooms, mince and sauté until golden brown. If using dried, pour boiling water over 1 ounce morels just to cover. Soak until soft, drain, and reserve soaking water. Finely mince morels and substitute soaking water for some of chicken stock. Sprinkle flour over, whisk in, and cook slowly for 5 minutes, stirring occasionally. Add wine, whisk to blend, and cook 3 minutes. Blend in chicken stock and cook, stirring often, until reduced by half and thickened. Blend in cream and cook slowly, stirring often, until smooth and satiny. Adjust seasonings with salt and pepper. Cover and set aside; keep warm.

Lightly pound chicken breasts or scallops. Dust with seasoned flour. Sauté lightly in butter and oil. Place on a warmed serving plate and pour morel sauce over.

## GARLAND'S
## APPLE CREAM SORBET

*Makes about 1-1/2 pints*
1 quart water
1 cup dry white wine
1 cup honey
1 cinnamon stick
1 teaspoon pure vanilla extract
6 large unpeeled cooking apples, cored and chopped
1/2 cup seedless raisins
1 cup heavy cream
Fresh mint

In a large saucepan, combine water, wine, honey, and cinnamon stick. Bring to a boil, add vanilla, and stir in apples and raisins. Bring back to a gentle boil, lower heat, cover, and simmer 1 hour, stirring occasionally. Cool and discard cinnamon stick. Purée in a food processor or blender and blend in cream. Freeze in a shallow dish until slushy. Whip with an electric mixer to fluff, and return to freezer. Repeat process and freeze. Serve in champagne glasses garnished with mint.

# GOLDEN HERB BRAIDS

*Makes two braids*

2 tablespoons (2 packages) active dry
 yeast
1/2 cup lukewarm water
1/4 cup boiling water
1/3 cup butter
1/3 cup firmly packed brown sugar
1/4 cup safflower oil
1/4 cup honey
3/4 tablespoon salt
4 eggs, lightly beaten
1/2 cup chopped fresh parsley
1 tablespoon chopped fresh basil
2 tablespoons chopped fresh chives
1 tablespoon finely minced fresh rosemary
3 cups whole-wheat flour
3-1/2 cups unbleached flour, or as needed
Egg Wash, following
Poppy or sesame seeds

In a small bowl, sprinkle yeast over lukewarm water, stir, and let stand until bubbly. In a large mixing bowl, combine boiling water, butter, sugar, oil, honey, and salt. Cool to lukewarm and blend in yeast mixture. Combine eggs and herbs and stir in. Gradually beat in whole-wheat flour and enough unbleached flour to make a soft dough. Turn out onto a floured board and knead 5 minutes, adding unbleached flour as needed to prevent sticking. Form into a ball, place in an oiled bowl, turn to coat all surfaces, cover with a tea towel and let rise in a warm place 1-1/2 hours or until doubled in bulk.

Punch down and divide dough in half. Working with one half at a time, divide into 3 equal portions. Roll each portion into a long rope. Pinch ends together and braid, tucking in bottom ends. Transfer to a greased cookie sheet and repeat with remaining dough. Cover with a tea towel and let rise in a warm place 40 minutes or until almost doubled in size.

Place braids in oven, turn heat to 350°F, and bake 20 minutes. Brush with egg wash and bake another 10 minutes until deeply golden. If braids appear to be browning too quickly, lightly cover with foil. Bread is done when it sounds hollow when tapped with fingertips. Remove to a wire rack and cool.

EGG WASH: Beat 1 egg white lightly with 1 tablespoon cold water.

# Harbor House
## Elk, California

South of Mendocino and below the village of Elk on California's rugged north coast is a former logging port known as Greenwood Landing. In 1916, during the height of the lumber boom, the Goodyear Redwood Lumber Company built a stately mansion here on the cliffs above the Pacific to be used as an executive residence. The house is now a popular inn owned and managed by former schoolteacher Patricia Corcoran. Her cooking is a highlight of a visit here, especially the bountiful dinners. The huge windows of the dining room overlook the garden, the source of the inn's vegetables. And below is the pounding surf, where the evening's fish probably swam the night before. The following recipes make up a typical meal at Harbor House. Ling cod and rock cod are indigenous to the Mendocino area; snapper may be substituted.

## BROCCOLI SOUP

*Serves ten*
4 bunches broccoli
3 quarts well-seasoned chicken broth, preferably homemade
2 cups heavy cream
Freshly ground pepper to taste
4 tablespoons butter
1/4 cup sesame seeds

Peel broccoli stems and cut stems and florets into small chunks. Add to broth, bring to a boil, lower heat slightly, cover, and cook until broccoli is very tender. Cool and purée a little at a time in a blender or food processor. Return to saucepan and add cream and pepper. In a small saucepan or skillet, melt butter and add sesame seeds. Cook, stirring, over medium heat until seeds just begin to brown. Add to soup, stir, and reheat; do not boil. Ladle into heated soup bowls.

## MUSHROOMS AU GRATIN

*Serves ten*
2 pounds firm mushrooms, cleaned and
   thinly sliced
1/4 pound butter
1 cup sour cream
1/4 cup minced fresh parsley
6 to 8 ounces Cheddar or Swiss cheese,
   grated (1-1/2 to 2 cups)

In a large skillet, sauté mushrooms in
butter 10 minutes, turning and stirring
often. Cool. Preheat oven to 350°F.
Blend sour cream and parsley into mushrooms. Transfer to a shallow baking dish
and sprinkle cheese over. Bake 15 minutes
or until bubbly.

## CELERY ROOT SALAD

*Serves ten*
7 medium celery roots, about 12 ounces
   each
1/2 bunch celery, thinly sliced or cut in
   julienne
1 bunch radishes, thinly sliced or cut in
   julienne
4 green onions, sliced or cut in julienne

DRESSING
1/2 cup good-quality white wine vinegar
   or champagne vinegar
2/3 cup safflower or soy oil
1 teaspoon salt
1/2 teaspoon freshly ground pepper

Lettuce leaves or bed of lettuce

Wash celery roots and cook in boiling
salted water to cover 30 minutes or until
just tender. Cool, peel, and slice thinly or
cut in julienne. Toss with celery, radishes,
and green onions. Combine dressing
ingredients, whisking to blend thoroughly.
Pour over vegetables, toss well, and chill
2 to 3 hours. Spoon onto lettuce leaves.

NOTE: This dressing is also excellent on
shredded green or red cabbage.

## CARROTS AND RED ONIONS

*Serves ten*
4 to 5 pounds carrots
5 small red onions
1/2 pound butter

Scrape or peel carrots and slice as thinly as possible on an extreme diagonal; set aside. Peel and thinly slice onions. In a large saucepan, melt butter. Stir in carrots and onions to coat well. Cover and cook over medium-low heat 10 minutes or until tender, stirring occasionally.

## MARINATED PACIFIC LING C

*Serves ten*
10 ling cod or rock cod fillets
Salt and freshly ground pepper

MARINADE
3 cups olive oil
1/4 cup prepared mustard
1/4 cup red wine vinegar
4 teaspoons prepared horseradish
2 teaspoons paprika
1/2 teaspoon curry powder
1/2 teaspoon cayenne pepper
4 teaspoons garlic juice

Approximately 2 cups dry bread crumbs

Lightly sprinkle fillets with salt and pepper. Place in a large shallow pan. In a large jar, combine marinade ingredients and shake well. Pour over fillets. Cover and let stand 2 to 3 hours, turning occasionally.
  Preheat broiler. One at a time, remove fillets from marinade and roll in bread crumbs. Place on a broiler rack and broil 4 minutes on each side or until fish flakes easily.

## MOCHA TOFFEE PIE

*Serves eight to ten*

CRUST
1/2 recipe pastry dough, page 152
1/4 cup firmly packed brown sugar
3/4 cup finely chopped walnuts
1/2 square (1/2 ounce) unsweetened
    chocolate, grated
1 teaspoon pure vanilla extract
1 tablespoon cold water

FILLING
1/2 square (1/2 ounce) unsweetened
    chocolate, grated
2 teaspoons instant coffee granules
1/4 pound chilled butter, cut up
3/4 cup granulated sugar
2 eggs

1 cup heavy cream
2 teaspoons instant coffee granules
1/4 cup powdered sugar
Milk chocolate curls

Preheat oven to 350°F. To prepare crust, crumble pastry dough into a large bowl. With a fork, stir in sugar, walnuts, and chocolate, combining well. Stir in vanilla and water and press into a well-buttered 9-inch pie tin. Bake 15 minutes, remove from oven, and cool.

To make filling, combine chocolate and coffee; set aside to cool. In bowl of an electric mixer beat butter until light and fluffy. Gradually add sugar, beating constantly. Blend in chocolate-coffee mixture. Add 1 egg and beat 5 minutes. Add remaining egg and beat 5 minutes. Turn into baked pie shell and chill 3 to 6 hours or overnight.

To serve, combine cream, coffee, and sugar and whip until stiff. Decorate pie with whipped cream and top with chocolate curls.

# Heritage House
*Little River, California*

The most luxurious inn on California's north coast, Heritage House is a complex of cottages rambling over hillsides, meadows, and gardens down to a private beach. The main building, which houses the large dining room and cocktail lounge, was built in 1876 by John Dennen, a former New Englander. His grandson, L. D. Dennen, started the inn in 1949 and over the years expanded the quaint overnight accommodations, in many cases moving old structures from nearby towns—a schoolhouse from Elk, a water tower from Mendocino—and converting them into guest houses. The cooking at Heritage House is basic American fare, some of it reflecting Dennen's New England heritage. The fresh seafood often served here is from the morning's catch at the fishing port of Noyo, north of Little River.

## RED SNAPPER
## WITH GINGER CREAM SAUCE

Start a day ahead so the ginger can be
soaked overnight.

*Serves four*

1/4 cup very thinly julienned peeled
    ginger root
1 cup Pinot Chardonnay or other dry
    white wine
2 tablespoons unsalted butter
2 tablespoons unbleached flour
1 cup heavy cream at room temperature
1/8 teaspoon freshly ground white pepper
Eight 8-ounce fillets of red snapper
2 egg yolks, lightly beaten
Salt to taste
Lemon wedges

Soak ginger root in wine overnight.
Drain ginger, reserving wine, and set
ginger aside. In a heavy saucepan, melt
butter and whisk in flour. Cook and stir
a few minutes and gradually whisk in
cream. Add pepper and reserved drained
ginger. Simmer over a heat deflector,
stirring occasionally, 45 minutes to 1
hour.

Preheat oven to 375°F. Trim bones
from fillets and place in a 9x13x2-nch
glass or enamel baking pan. Add reserved
wine from soaking ginger. Cover tightly
with aluminum foil and bake about 20
minutes or until fish flakes easily when
prodded with a fork. Drain liquid from
pan and cover fillets; keep warm. Measure
1/2 cup of liquid and whisk into egg
yolks. Whisk this mixture into cream
sauce. Season with salt and simmer,
stirring, 5 minutes. Ladle sauce over fish
and serve with lemon wedges.

## BOURBON-BRAISED PORK LOIN

*Serves four to six*
One 5- to 6-pound pork loin
Dijon-style mustard
Brown sugar
1/2 cup Jim Beam or other good bourbon

BOURBON SAUCE
1 large carrot, finely diced
1 large onion, finely diced
1 celery stalk, finely diced
3 to 4 tablespoons butter
1 cup dry white wine
4 cups strong beef or veal stock
*Bouquet garni,* page 151
3 tablespoons White Roux, page 151
Pan drippings from roast
1/4 cup Jim Beam or other good bourbon
2 tablespoons butter (optional)

Preheat oven to 400°F. Coat pork roast lightly with mustard and brown sugar. Place in a shallow baking pan and roast 15 minutes. Heat bourbon to boiling, pour over loin, and ignite. Let flames die down. Reduce oven temperature to 325°F and roast loin 18 minutes per pound. Let rest 15 to 20 minutes before carving.

While pork is roasting, prepare sauce: In a heavy skillet, brown vegetables in 3 to 4 tablespoons butter. Deglaze skillet with wine and reduce until almost evaporated. Add stock and *bouquet garni.* Stir in roux and simmer, stirring occasionally, 1 hour. When roast is cooked, add drippings from pan. Simmer 10 minutes and strain. Add bourbon, heat, skim if necessary, and swirl in butter, if desired.

## MANDARIN ZABAGLIONE CREAM IN ORANGE CUPS

*Serves six*
3 egg yolks
1/4 cup granulated sugar
1/2 cup Grand Marnier
2 cups heavy cream
1/4 to 1/2 cup granulated sugar
1 cup chopped well-drained mandarin
   oranges
2 tablespoons freshly grated orange rind
3 oranges
Grated orange rind
Mint leaves

In a stainless steel bowl, whisk egg yolks and sugar until thick and lemon colored. Place bowl over simmering water and whisk in Grand Marnier. Continue whisking until mixture is consistency of soft custard. Remove from heat, let stand a few minutes, and whisk again. Set in a cool place.

Whip cream until stiff and gently mix in sugar to taste. Fold in mandarin oranges and 2 tablespoons orange rind. Gently fold in the cool Grand Marnier mixture. Halve oranges and scoop out the sections and white membrane. Cut a zigzag pattern on top edges. Spoon *zabaglione* mixture into them and chill 4 to 6 hours. Garnish with grated orange rind and mint leaves.

## OLD-FASHIONED MOLASSES-GRANOLA BREAD

*Makes two loaves*

1-1/2 tablespoons (1-1/2 packages) active
   dry yeast
1/4 cup lukewarm water
1 cup milk, scalded
2 tablespoons butter
1 cup water
2 tablespoons granulated sugar
1/4 cup unsulphured dark molasses
1 tablespoon salt
2 teaspoons ground allspice
1 teaspoon grated nutmeg
5 cups unbleached flour, or as needed
2 cups unsweetened granola
1 teaspoon pure vanilla extract
1 teaspoon pure almond extract

TOPPING
2 tablespoons unbleached flour
2 tablespoons granulated sugar
3 tablespoons brown sugar
1/2 teaspoon ground cinnamon
1/2 teaspoon grated nutmeg
2 tablespoons butter, cut up
1/3 cup unprocessed rolled oats or
   chopped nuts

1 egg white, lightly beaten

Sprinkle yeast over lukewarm water, stir, and let stand until bubbly. In a large bowl, combine milk and butter, stir to melt butter, and add water, sugar, molasses, salt, and spices. Cool to lukewarm and stir in yeast mixture. Gradually beat in 2 cups of flour, granola, vanilla extract, and almond extract. Gradually beat in remaining flour to make a stiff dough. Turn out onto a lightly floured board and knead 3 minutes, adding additional flour only as needed to prevent sticking. Lightly oil hands and board and continue kneading, without adding more flour, 5 to 6 minutes. Dough will be slightly sticky because of the granola.

Form dough into a ball, place in an oiled bowl, turn to coat all surfaces, cover with a tea towel, and let rise in warm place 1-1/2 hours or until double in bulk. Punch down, form into 2 loaves, and place in buttered or oiled 9x5x3-inch loaf pans. Cover with a tea towel and let rise in a warm place 45 minutes or until almost double in size.

While dough is rising the second time, make topping: Combine flour, sugars, and spices. Crumble in butter and toss in oats; set aside. Preheat oven to 325°F. Brush loaves with egg white and sprinkle with topping. Bake 40 minutes or until loaves are browned and sound hollow when tapped with fingers. Turn out onto a wire rack, turn right side up, and cool.

## Magnolia Hotel
### Napa Valley, California

The early settlers of the Napa Valley, California's most famous wine-producing area, were German, French, and Italian winemakers who discovered that the European *vinifera* grapes would flourish in the valley's fertile soil and on the surrounding rocky hillsides. The valley's first settlement was Yountville, named after George Yount, who was given an eleven-thousand-acre tract of land by his friend General Mariano Guadalupe Vallejo, commander of the Mexican troops based in nearby Sonoma. In 1873 a three-story stone hotel was built in Yountville; travelers were charged a dollar a night for a room. At one time during its long history the hotel was reputedly a brothel, and during Prohibition it was indisputedly a center for bootleggers. In 1968 Ray and Nancy Monte restored the hotel in late nineteenth-century style. Then in 1977 Bruce Locken, former general manager of the Clift Hotel in San Francisco, and his wife Bonnie took over. On weekends Bonnie cooks spectacular dinners in a small candlelit restaurant adjoining the hotel. Her elegant Continental cuisine reflects the valley's heritage and has earned her a number of *Holiday* awards.

## AVOCADO SOUP

*Serves six*
2 ripe avocados, cut in chunks
1 green onion, sliced
3 cups rich chicken broth
1 cup heavy cream
Salt and freshly ground white pepper to
    taste
2 tablespoons minced fresh dill

Purée avocados in a food processor or
blender. Add green onion and purée
thoroughly. Add broth and blend. Remove
to a bowl and blend in cream, salt, and
pepper. Chill thoroughly. Serve in chilled
bowls, sprinkled with dill.

## MARINATED
## FRESH MUSHROOM SALAD

*Serves four*
1 pound mushrooms, sliced
Juice of 1 large lemon

MARINADE
1/2 cup safflower or corn oil
2 tablespoons olive oil
1 tablespoon Dijon-style mustard
2 tablespoons white wine tarragon vinegar
1 teaspoon granulated sugar
1/2 cup chopped green onions
2 tablespoons chopped fresh parsley
Salt and freshly ground pepper to taste

Butter lettuce leaves

Toss mushrooms with lemon juice to
prevent browning. Blend marinade ingredients thoroughly and toss with mushrooms.
Chill. To serve, mound on lettuce leaves.

## ROAST RACK OF LAMB MAGNOLIA

*Serves six*
1 double rack of lamb (6 to 8 pounds),
    split
Safflower or corn oil for searing
1 carrot, sliced
1 onion, chopped
1 garlic clove, crushed
1 bay leaf
1 cup dry white wine
1 cup dry bread crumbs
6 tablespoons butter
3 shallots, finely minced
1/2 cup chopped fresh parsley
1/2 teaspoon crushed fresh thyme

Preheat oven to 350°F. Trim rack of lamb and wrap ends of ribs in foil to prevent burning. Sear on all sides in oil. Place in roasting pan and arrange vegetables around meat. Pour in wine and roast 35 to 45 minutes to medium rare, basting with juices every 10 minutes.

While lamb is roasting, brown crumbs in butter. Add shallots and sauté 5 minutes. Add parsley and thyme and mix well. When lamb is done, pat crumb mixture firmly on top and return to oven for 5 minutes. Remove from oven and let rest 10 minutes before carving. Strain pan juices and serve as gravy.

## RASPBERRY BAVARIAN PIE

*Makes one 10-inch pie*

PASTRY SHELL
4 tablespoons butter
2 tablespoons granulated sugar
1/4 teaspoon salt
1 egg yolk
3/4 cup unbleached flour
1/3 cup finely chopped almonds

FILLING
One 10-ounce package frozen raspberries
2 egg whites
1 cup granulated sugar
1 tablespoon fresh lemon juice
1/3 teaspoon pure vanilla extract
Pinch salt
1 cup heavy cream
Heavy cream, whipped
Fresh raspberries (optional)

To make pastry shell, preheat oven to 400°F. Cream butter, sugar, and salt until fluffy. Add egg yolk and beat well. Mix in flour and almonds and press into a 10-inch pie pan. Bake 10 minutes, remove to a wire rack, and cool.

To make filling, place raspberries, egg whites, sugar, lemon juice, vanilla, and salt in bowl of mixer. Beat *15 minutes*. While mixture is mixing, beat cream until soft peaks form. Fold in raspberry mixture and pile into prepared pastry shell. Freeze. When ready to serve, decorate with dollops of whipped cream and fresh raspberries.

## Manka's/Inverness Lodge
### Inverness, California

The so-called "California cuisine" is an ethnic hodgepodge based on the state's heritage of many nationalities. French, Italian, and Oriental influences prevail, but here and there you can find a trace of almost every country's cooking. The resort village of Inverness, on the shores of Tomales Bay north of San Francisco, has become a bastion of Czech cooking with the town's two best restaurants offering that fare. One of these is Manka's, the creation of Czech emigrés Manka and Milan Prokupek, who took over the rustic Inverness Lodge in 1956. Soon their meals were attracting diners from all over the San Francisco Bay Area. Today Manka still bakes the rich Czech-Viennese pastries that conclude the hearty meals, but most of the cooking is done by her daughter-in-law Judy Prokupek. Dinner here starts with a visit to a lavish buffet table laden with Danish cheeses, sausages, cold meats, fresh fruit, relishes, several salads, and Norwegian herring. The following meal is created around oysters, the seafood for which Tomales Bay is famous.

## LENTIL SOUP

*Serves six to eight*
3 cups dried lentils
4 to 6 slices bacon
2 tablespoons butter
1 onion, diced
2 carrots, diced
1 parsnip, diced
1 turnip, diced
6 garlic cloves, minced
2 quarts ham stock or water
1 tablespoon minced fresh marjoram
Salt and freshly ground pepper to taste
Dark rye croûtons

Soak lentils in water to cover 1 to 2 hours; drain. Cut bacon into strips and cook until browned. Remove with slotted spoon, drain on paper towels, and reserve. Add butter to skillet and lightly brown vegetables and garlic. In a soup kettle, heat stock. Add vegetables, lentils, and marjoram. Cover, bring to a boil, lower heat, and cook slowly 30 minutes or until lentils have completely softened. Season with salt and pepper and add bacon. Serve with dark rye croûtons.

## OYSTERS WITH ANCHOVY BUTTER

*Serves six*

ANCHOVY BUTTER
1 pound butter at room temperature
12 anchovy fillets
2 egg yolks
1 whole egg
4 garlic cloves, finely minced
2 tablespoons chopped fresh parsley
1/2 medium onion, finely diced
2 tablespoons crumbled dried tarragon
1/3 cup dry white wine
1/8 teaspoon freshly ground pepper

Oysters in the shell (at least 6 per serving)
Rock salt
1/4 to 1/2 cup fine dry bread crumbs

Preheat oven to 400°F. Combine Anchovy Butter ingredients thoroughly. Shuck oysters, reserving half of shells. Arrange oyster shells in a shallow pan on a bed of rock salt. Place 1 or 2 oysters in each shell. Cover with a spoonful of Anchovy Butter. Bake 20 minutes. Lightly sprinkle bread crumbs over oysters and return to oven for 3 to 5 minutes or until browned.

NOTE: Do not add any salt to this recipe.

## NUT TORTE

*Makes one torte*
5 egg whites
1 cup granulated sugar
1 tablespoon pure vanilla extract
1-3/4 cups chopped walnuts or hazelnuts
Grated peel of 1 lemon
2 tablespoons fine dry bread crumbs
About 3/4 cup heavy cream
Powdered sugar to taste
Chopped walnuts or hazelnuts
Grated semisweet chocolate

Oil two 9-inch spring-form pans (see Baking Hints, page 153) and cover bottoms with circles of parchment paper. Oil paper and set pans aside. Preheat oven to 250°F. Beat egg whites until stiff but not dry. Gradually beat in sugar and beat until peaks form and mixture is glossy. Fold in vanilla. Combine nuts, lemon peel, and bread crumbs. Gently fold in and carefully spread mixture in prepared pans. Bake 1 to 1-1/2 hours or until completely dry. Cool on wire rack and gently remove from pans.

To assemble torte, place 1 layer on a serving plate. Whip cream, adding powdered sugar to taste. Spread bottom layer with whipped cream and place second layer on top. Spread with a thin coating of whipped cream. Using a pastry bag, pipe rosettes and a border on torte to decorate. Sprinkle with chopped nuts and grated chocolate.

## Pelican Inn
### Muir Beach, California

British fare is rightfully the first northern California cuisine, according to English-born Charles Felix, owner of the Pelican Inn. He bases this belief on Sir Francis Drake's visit to Pacific shores in 1579, when he claimed California for Queen Elizabeth I and her descendants forever.

To help carry out this mandate, Felix built a replica of a sixteenth-century English farmhouse on the edge of the Pacific and named the inn Pelican—the original name of Drake's ship, later called *Golden Hinde*. The dining room is a re-creation of a typical English pub, serving shepherd pies, Scotch eggs, bangers, and the like—recipes from a pub that four generations of Felix's family operated in England.

## CHILLED MULLIGATAWNY SOUP

Mulligatawny soup—a favorite among the British in India, and brought home by them—is a rich meat stock strongly flavored with curry. This version transforms the traditional hot soup into a cool summer starter.

*Serves six*
1 onion, finely chopped
1 carrot, finely chopped
2 tablespoons unsalted butter
3 tablespoons unbleached flour
2 to 2-1/2 teaspoons curry powder
5 cups hot beef stock
2 tablespoons mango liquid (unsweetened juice)
Cauliflower, divided into florets

Sauté onion and carrot in butter until onion is translucent. Sift flour and curry powder together and sprinkle over vegetables. Stirring constantly, cook over medium heat until mixture is a deep brown color. Gradually stir in hot stock and bring to a boil. Stirring occasionally, simmer over low heat 30 minutes. Cool slightly and purée in a blender or food processor, or force through coarse sieve. Stir in mango liquid and chill at least 2 hours. Before serving, remove any fat from surface, pour into 6 bowls, and garnish with cauliflower.

## RAISED PORK PIE

The hot-water crust used for this classic English pie is the earliest known form of pastry case. It dates back to the fourteenth century and has found its perpetuity in the famous Melton Mowbray pork pie. The pastry is traditionally molded around a floured jar, but special molds are now available and may be used instead of a jar.

*Serves four to six*

PASTRY CRUST
3 cups unbleached flour
1/4 teaspoon salt
1/4 cup milk
1/4 cup water
4 tablespoons lard
Boiling water if needed
1 to 1-1/2 cups rich gelatinous pork, veal, or beef stock, chilled
1 teaspoon unflavored gelatin if needed
1-1/2 pounds lean pork
Salt and freshly ground black pepper to taste
2 tablespoons cold water
1 small egg, lightly beaten

To make pastry, heavily butter bottom and outside of a 1-quart wide-mouthed canning jar. Generously sprinkle with flour and set aside upside down. Have a double boiler over boiling water ready. Sift flour and salt. In a large saucepan, bring milk, water, and lard to a boil, stirring to melt lard. Remove from heat and add flour all at once. Stir quickly until mixture forms a smooth, soft dough, adding a few drops of boiling water if dough is too stiff. Cut off one third of dough and place in double boiler. Quickly mold remaining dough around prepared jar, enclosing jar up to about 2 inches from top with a casing of dough approximately 1/4 inch thick. If dough dries out or starts to crack, place on a plate over boiling water to soften. When jar is encased, let dry for 10 minutes.

Check stock to see if it has set to a gelatinous state. If not, soften gelatin in 2 tablespoons of the stock, bring remaining stock to a boil, stir in gelatin mixture to dissolve gelatin, and set aside. Remove all excess fat from pork and cut meat into 1/2-inch cubes. Season with salt and pepper; stir in water.

When crust has set, gently remove from jar by loosening it with a spatula, keeping crust in shape. Preheat oven to 375°F. Place on a work surface and carefully pack in meat mixture to within 3/4 inch from top. Roll out reserved pastry to make a lid, moisten pie edge with cold water, put lid into position, and press edges tightly together to seal. Make a hole in top of pie and wrap bottom and sides in buttered parchment paper, securing with twine. Place on a lightly greased baking sheet and brush top with beaten egg. Bake 1 hour, reduce heat to 350°F, and bake 1 hour longer. If top seems to be browning too quickly, loosely cover with aluminum foil.

Remove pie from oven and let it cool almost completely. While it is cooling, reheat stock, adjust seasonings, and, when pie is cooled, carefully and slowly, using a small funnel, pour stock into hole in top of pie. Tip occasionally to let stock absorb. Continue until as much stock as possible has been added. Refrigerate several hours while stock sets to a jelly. Remove parchment paper and serve cold, cut into wedges.

SYLLABUB

*Serves four*
4 egg yolks
1/16 teaspoon ground cinnamon
1 teaspoon granulated sugar
2 teaspoons Grand Marnier or sweet
   sherry
4 ounces strawberries, mashed
   (approximately 1/2 cup mashed)
Whole strawberries and/or halved ladyfingers

In a medium-sized bowl, lightly beat eggs and cinnamon. Place bowl over a saucepan of boiling water, turn heat off and beat yolk mixture until fluffy and just starting to cook. Never stop beating or yolks will set. Beat in sugar and then Grand Marnier. Continue beating until fluffy and stiff. (The British call this the "balloon stage.") Immediately remove from heat and quickly fold in mashed strawberries. Pour into four champagne glasses, cover with foil, and refrigerate. When ready to serve, decorate with whole strawberries and/or halved ladyfingers.

# San Benito House
## Half Moon Bay, California

San Benito is the original Spanish name of Half Moon Bay, a coastal village just south of San Francisco. Here a turn-of-the-century hotel was operated for many years under the name Dominic's, and, though the building was run-down, huge, bargain-priced Italian dinners attracted crowds from many miles around. In 1976, Carol Regan, a schoolteacher and dedicated cook, bought the small hotel, restored it in a carefree country style, and renamed it San Benito House. Now the inn's dining room, picture pretty with glass doors leading to a flower-filled deck, attracts more visitors from greater distances than ever before. Carol's cooking ranges from country French to northern Italian, and she relies heavily on the bounty of the area: pumpkins and artichokes from the fields surrounding Half Moon Bay, and fish from the nearby harbor of Princeton. The following menu might best be described as San Francisco Italian because it centers around Crab Cioppino, the seafood stew created by the Italian fisherman who settled in the city by the Golden Gate.

110

## ARTICHOKES ALLA ROMANA

*Serves eight*
8 medium artichokes
Fresh lemon juice
1/2 cup finely chopped fresh Italian
  parsley
1 tablespoon garlic purée
2 tablespoons finely chopped fresh mint
1 teaspoon salt
Several grinds of fresh black pepper
3/4 cup good-quality olive oil
Chicken stock

Trim artichokes of all tough outer leaves, leaving only pale yellow leaves and 1-1/2 inches of stem. Rub with lemon juice as you work to prevent discoloration. Scoop out inner choke. Combine parsley, garlic, mint, salt, and pepper and stuff 1 teaspoonful into each center. Rub mixture well into sides, place artichokes base side down in a heavy casserole or saucepan (not cast iron or aluminum), and sprinkle remaining herb mixture over them. Pour olive oil over and add enough stock to reach one third of the way up artichokes. Cover with buttered parchment paper or brown paper and bring to boil. Reduce heat and cover with lid. Cook 30 minutes or until just tender when pierced with a fork. Serve at room temperature or chilled.

111

# FETTUCCINE WITH PESTO SAUCE

*Serves five to six*

PESTO SAUCE
2 cups fresh basil leaves
1/2 cup olive oil
2 large garlic cloves, pressed
1 teaspoon salt
1/2 cup freshly grated Parmesan cheese
2 to 3 tablespoons freshly grated Romano
   cheese
Freshly ground pepper to taste

4 quarts water
2 tablespoons salt
1-1/2 pounds fresh *fettuccine*
2 to 3 tablespoons butter, softened

Additional grated Parmesan and/or
   Romano cheese

To make sauce, in a blender or food processor purée basil, oil, garlic, and salt. Stir in cheeses and pepper (or save pepper to grind at table).

Bring water and salt to a rolling boil. Toss *fettuccine* with hands to separate and, keeping water at a boil, slowly drop into water. It will be done in 30 to 60 seconds; if homemade, within 15 seconds. Watch carefully; the pasta should be cooked *al dente*. Drain immediately and place in heated serving dish. Stir in butter and pour Pesto Sauce over. Sprinkle with grated cheese and serve with a bowl of grated cheese.

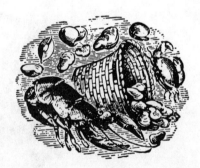

## CRAB CIOPPINO

*Serves six*

1/2 cup chopped green onions, white
    parts only
3 tablespoons olive oil
6 shallots, finely chopped
5 large tomatoes, peeled, seeded, and
    chopped
2 large garlic cloves, pressed
3 tablespoons chopped fresh Italian
    parsley
2 tablespoons chopped fresh dill or
    oregano
1/2 bay leaf
4 tablespoons tomato paste (optional)
1 quart Fish Stock, following, or bottled
    clam juice
Salt to taste
1 package Crab Boil
4 to 6 fresh Dungeness crabs

Sauté onions in oil until translucent. Add shallots, tomatoes, garlic, and herbs. Simmer 30 minutes. If tomatoes need flavor and body, add tomato paste and mix well. Stir in fish stock and salt; simmer 30 minutes. While sauce is simmering, bring a large kettle of water to boil. Mix in Crab Boil and drop crabs in. After water comes back to a full boil, cook for 14 minutes. Remo[...] ately; crabs should be slightly [...] because they will be cooked [...] sauce.

When cool enough to handle, and working over a bowl to catch juices and crab butter, remove claws and legs. Pull backs off and break bodies in half. Do not wash crabs. Stir juices and crab butter into sauce and add crab pieces. Reheat and serve immediately.

FISH STOCK
*Makes one quart*
2 pounds non-oily fish bones, shells, skins
2 cups water
2 cups dry white wine
6 parsley stems
1 bay leaf
1/2 cup chopped celery leaves

In a large kettle, combine ingredients and bring to a boil. Skim off any scum that appears on surface, cover, lower heat, and simmer 20 minutes. Strain, pour into a jar, and cool. Cover and refrigerate not more than two days.

# CHOCOLATE AMARETTO TORTE

This dessert appears complicated, but is so delicious it is worth the effort. The chocolate *génoise* may be made a day ahead and wrapped in foil. The *vacherin* layer may also be made ahead and stored in an airtight tin. This recipe makes three meringues—freeze two for future use. Even the butter cream may be made in advance, refrigerated or frozen, and brought to room temperature before using. (Carol suggests doubling or tripling the butter cream recipe and keeping it on hand in the freezer for other desserts.) Assemble the torte just before serving.

*Makes one torte*

CHOCOLATE GENOISE
4 tablespoons unsalted butter
1 teaspoon pure vanilla extract
4 eggs
2/3 cup granulated sugar
1/2 cup sifted unbleached flour, sifted
    together with
1/2 cup sifted unsweetened cocoa

To make *génoise,* oil an 8-inch round cake pan (see Baking Hints, page 153) and line with parchment paper. Oil paper and set pan aside. Preheat oven to 350°F. Clarify butter (see page 151), remove from heat, and stir in vanilla. Set aside to cool to lukewarm. In top of a double boiler, beat eggs until lemon colored. Beat in sugar until fluffy and smooth. Over simmering water, beat with an electric beater until thickened to consistency of softly whipped cream. Remove from heat. Fold one third of dry ingredients into egg mixture. Working quickly but gently, fold in rest of dry ingredients. Scoop about one fourth of batter into a separate bowl and blend in butter and vanilla mixture. Fold into rest of batter and pour into prepared pan. Bake 30 to 45 minutes or until cake shrinks away from sides of pan and center top springs back when touched with finger. Cool on a wire rack 15 minutes and turn out onto rack to finish cooling.

VACHERIN LAYER
6 egg whites
Pinch salt
1 teaspoon fresh lemon juice
1-1/4 cups granulated sugar
2 teaspoons pure vanilla extract
1 cup ground almonds

To make *vacherin* layer, oil a large cookie sheet. Cut out three 8-inch parchment paper circles and arrange on sheet. Oil circles (see note on meringues, page 153). Preheat oven to 325°F. Beat egg whites and salt to soft-peak stage. Add lemon juice and gradually beat in sugar until whites are glossy and form stiff peaks. Fold in vanilla and then almonds. Divide meringue among parchment paper circles, smoothing gently to cover evenly and smoothly. Bake 30 to 45 minutes or until layers are crisp and lightly browned. Cool on a wire rack and carefully remove parchment paper.

CHOCOLATE BUTTER CREAM
4 squares (4 ounces) semisweet chocolate
1-1/2 tablespoons butter
3/4 cup granulated sugar
3/8 cup water (6 tablespoons)
1/8 teaspoon cream of tartar
1 egg
1 egg yolk
3/4 cup unsalted butter

To make butter cream, in top of a double boiler over simmering water melt chocolate and butter. In a saucepan (copper preferred), combine sugar, water, and cream of tartar. Cover and bring to a boil, stirring to dissolve sugar. Simmer, covered, 5 minutes. Uncover and cook, stirring occasionally, until syrup reaches 242°F. While syrup is cooking, beat egg and egg yolk until lemon colored and fluffy. When syrup is ready, start beating eggs again and slowly pour syrup in. Continue beating until mixture cools. Add unsalted butter and chocolate mixture. Set aside to cool.

SIMPLE SYRUP
2 cups granulated sugar
1 cup water
1/4 teaspoon cream of tartar
1/4 cup Amaretto, or to taste

To make simple syrup, in a saucepan combine sugar, water, and cream of tartar. Cover and bring to simmer, stirring to dissolve sugar, for 5 minutes. Uncover, cool, and store. When ready to use, add Amaretto.

To assemble torte, cut *génoise* into 2 layers (see page 153). With a spoon, ladle syrup over both layers. Place 1 layer on a serving plate. Spread with butter cream. Place a meringue circle on butter cream and top with second cake layer. Frost entire torte with butter cream.

# Union Hotel
*Los Alamos, California*

Built in 1880 as a Wells Fargo stage stop on the road from Santa Barbara to San Francisco, this hotel subsequently burned down, was rebuilt and later modernized, and finally in 1972 was restored by Dick Langdon to its 1880s character. The most modern thing about the place is probably a 1918 touring car used to transport overnight guests around the sleepy little agricultural town of Los Alamos. Langdon spent a year traveling around the United States to find antiques for his hotel, and in the big dining room he has installed furnishings and gaslights from a plantation in Mississippi. Dick's wife Teri is in charge of the meals, which feature family-style country cooking with some recipes derived from a nineteenth-century cookbook. A typical dinner at the hotel starts with Cheddar cheese and crackers, then a big tureen of Leather Apron Soup (a recipe used on the wagon trains that came to California), a salad of greens with a cheese dressing, and corn bread with honey butter. Next come platters of country-baked chicken, beef short ribs, boiled potatoes with lemon butter, and Chinese vegetables. Fruit fritters are a popular dessert.

## LEATHER APRON SOUP

*Serves six*
6 cups well-seasoned chicken broth
2/3 cup diced cooked chicken
1/4 cup diced onion
1 to 2 carrots, scraped and diced
1 to 2 celery stalks, diced
1 teaspoon minced fresh basil
1/4 teaspoon freshly ground white pepper

APRONS
1/2 cup unbleached flour
1/4 teaspoon salt
About 2 tablespoons cold water, or as
　needed

Place broth, chicken, vegetables, and seasonings in a large kettle and place over high heat. While mixture heats to a boil prepare Aprons: Combine flour and salt. With fork, stir in water, adding enough so that dough can be formed into a ball. Dough will be quite stiff. On a lightly floured board, roll out 1/8 inch thick. Cut into 1/2- to 3/4-inch squares.

One at a time, drop Aprons into boiling soup. Cover with tilted lid, lower heat slightly, and cook at a gentle boil 20 minutes. Serve at once in heated soup bowls.

## BEEF SHORT RIBS

*Serves six*
5 pounds beef short ribs
1 tablespoon lemon pepper
2 teaspoons garlic salt
1 teaspoon freshly ground black pepper

Preheat oven to 400°F. Place ribs in a deep baking pan, sprinkle seasonings over meat, cover with water, and cover pan with foil. Bake 1-1/2 to 3-1/2 hours or until tender. Cooking time depends on the cut of short ribs and the type of pan used. A Dutch oven will cook ribs more quickly. A kosher cut of very large ribs may take the full cooking time.

## BOILED POTATOES WITH LEMON BUTTER

*Serves six*
Boiling water to cover
4 baking potatoes, peeled and cut into
  thirds
1 teaspoon salt
1/4 pound butter, melted
1/4 cup fresh lemon juice
1 tablespoon minced fresh parsley

In a saucepan pour boiling water over
potatoes to cover, add salt, cover, bring
back to a gentle boil, and cook 15 to 20
minutes or until potatoes are tender.
Drain thoroughly. Combine butter, lemon
juice, and parsley. Pour over potatoes
and serve at once.

NOTE: Scrubbed unpeeled new potatoes
may be substituted for the baking potatoes.

## BLACKBERRY FRITTERS

*Serves six*
2 cups unbleached flour
1 tablespoon baking powder
1 teaspoon salt
1/4 cup granulated sugar
2 eggs, lightly beaten
1 cup milk
2 cups fresh blackberries
Peanut oil for deep-frying
Powdered sugar

Fill a fryer or a deep, heavy saucepan
with oil to at least 6 inches. Heat oil to
375°F. Combine flour, baking powder,
salt, and sugar. Stir in eggs and milk;
blend and fold in berries. Working with
4 to 6 spoonfuls at a time, depending on
size of pan, drop into hot oil and cook,
turning once, 2 to 3 minutes or until
golden. Drain on paper toweling and
keep warm if not serving at once. Repeat
with remaining batter. Sieve powdered
sugar over and serve immediately.

NOTE: Fresh or frozen blueberries or
raspberries may be substituted for blackberries. Cooked apples or fresh strawberries or peaches may also be substituted.

# Vineyard House
## Coloma, California

James W. Marshall discovered California's first gold in Coloma on January 24, 1848. The town quickly grew to ten thousand inhabitants, but by 1868 the gold was depleted and only a few hundred people remained. Ten years later Robert Chalmers, an extravagant local vintner, built a nineteen-room mansion with nine fire-places just outside of the town. Here he once staged a banquet in Marshall's memory for two thousand guests. A century later the Vineyard House had deteriorated into a rundown hotel, but in 1975 Frank and Darlene Herrera and David Van-Buskirk bought the place and restored it in the mood of the gold rush era. The restaurant, with its old-fashioned kerosene-burning lamps, provides some of the best country cooking in California's gold country. The house specialty is an individual pot of chicken simmering in sauce, topped with a two-inch layer of dumplings. The following recipe is a simplified version.

## PORTUGUESE BLACK BEAN SOUP

*Serves four for main meal, six as first course*
1/2 pound (about 1-1/2 cups) black beans
6 cups cold water
3/4 teaspoon salt
2 teaspoons cider vinegar
3/4 cup chopped onion
1 medium bell pepper, diced
1/2 cup chopped celery
1 medium carrot, thinly sliced
1 medium potato, diced
1 linguiça sausage, chopped, **or**
Leftover beef scraps
8 ounces (1 cup) tomato paste
3 garlic cloves, minced
2 cups water
1-1/2 tablespoons beef stock concentrate or
3 beef bouillon cubes
3/4 teaspoon ground cumin
1/2 teaspoon freshly ground black pepper
Dash cayenne pepper

In a large soup kettle, combine beans, cold water, salt, and vinegar. Bring to a boil, lower heat, and cook gently, uncovered, 45 minutes. Add remaining ingredients, bring back to a boil, reduce heat to a simmer and cook partially covered 1 hour or until beans are tender. Time will depend on individual taste. Stir occasionally while cooking. Before serving, adjust seasonings.

# CHICKEN AND DUMPLINGS

*Serves three to four*
One 2-1/2- to 3-pound chicken
1 quart chicken stock
1 stalk celery, cut up
1/2 onion, cut up
1/2 teaspoon salt
2 garlic cloves, minced
1/2 teaspoon poultry seasoning
Pinch ground allspice
1 cup chopped celery
1 cup chopped onion
1/4 cup grated carrot

DUMPLINGS

1-1/3 cups biscuit mix (Pillsbury preferred)
1/2 tablespoon crumbled dried basil
1/3 cup cold water

In a large saucepan, place chicken, chicken stock, celery, onion, salt, garlic, poultry seasoning, and allspice. Add water to almost cover chicken and bring to a boil. Cover, lower heat, and simmer, turning chicken several times, 30 minutes or until chicken is almost tender. Remove chicken from pot and set aside. Strain broth, pour into a jar, cool, cover, and refrigerate. Debone chicken, remove skin, and place chicken pieces in a saucepan or a straight-sided skillet with tight-fitting *rounded* lid. Add chopped celery, chopped onion, and carrots. Remove fat from broth and add 2 cups broth to vegetables and chicken, reserving remaining broth for soups or sauces. Bring to boil, cover, lower heat, and simmer 10 minutes.

When vegetables are almost tender, prepare dumplings. Combine biscuit mix and basil. With a fork, stir in water. Do not overmix. Spoon out 3 or 4 equal-sized amounts of mixture on top of broth, spacing evenly. Cover and simmer, without peeking, 10 to 15 minutes. Dumplings are done when a cake tester or toothpick inserted in center comes out clean. Spoon chicken and dumplings onto serving plates and spoon extra gravy over.

# THE NORTHWEST

*Oregon & Washington*

## *Wolf Creek Tavern*
*Wolf Creek, Oregon*

In the mountains of southern Oregon, not far from the Rogue River, Wolf Creek Tavern was built as a stagecoach stop in the 1870s—one of many inns that sprang up along the busy seven-hundred-mile wagon road from Sacramento to Portland. The tavern's early history is obscure; some say that Chinese laborers built it over the tailings of an old gold mine. But the inn has operated continu-ously under many owners, one of the most auspicious being John L. Dougall, who brought to it during the 1920s a reputation for fine cooking. The guests who have enjoyed the inn's hospitality reputedly include President Rutherford B. Hayes, Jack London, Sinclair Lewis, and Mary Pickford. Today the tavern is owned by the Oregon State Parks and Recreation Division, which leases it to innkeepers Vernon and Donna Ward. Vernon, as chef, carries the inn's tradition of good dining, with an emphasis on seafood.

## DUNGENESS CRAB BISQUE

*Serves six to ten*
1-1/2 quarts whole milk
1 teaspoon salt
1/2 teaspoon freshly ground white pepper
3 tablespoons White Roux (page 151)
  made with rendered chicken fat
6 ounces flaked crab meat
1/2 cup dry sherry
Heavy cream (optional)

In top of a double boiler over simmering water, combine and heat milk, salt, and pepper. Add roux, stirring and cooking until thickened to desired consistency. Add crab meat, sherry, and optional cream. Reheat and serve in heated soup bowls.

## SCALLOPS

*Serves two*
1/2 pound scallops
1 small garlic clove, crushed
2 tablespoons clarified butter (see page 151)
2 tablespoons extra-dry vermouth
1/2 tablespoon fresh lemon juice

Sauté scallops and garlic lightly in butter over medium heat; do *not* overcook. Scallops should just become opaque. Add vermouth, bring just to a boil, and add lemon juice. Serve immediately.

## CARROT CAKE

*Makes one cake*
2 cups unbleached flour
2 teaspoons baking powder
1/2 tablespoon baking soda
1 teaspoon ground cinnamon
1 teaspoon salt
2 cups granulated sugar
4 eggs
1-1/2 cups safflower oil
One 8-ounce can crushed pineapple,
  well drained
2 tablespoons pineapple juice
2 cups grated raw carrots
1 cup chopped walnuts, pecans, or filberts

Preheat oven to 350°F. Sift dry ingredients together. In a large bowl, beat eggs lightly and blend in oil, pineapple, pineapple juice, and carrots. Add dry ingredients and blend *just* until moistened. Fold in nuts and pour into a buttered and lightly floured 11x7x2-inch baking pan. Bake 35 minutes or until cake starts to shrink away from sides of pan and a cake tester inserted in center comes out clean. Place on a cooling rack and let cool. Serve from baking pan.

## Columbia Gorge Hotel
### Hood River, Oregon

In the early 1900s the beautiful Columbia River Valley, east of Portland, was a lush wilderness. All this was changed by millionaire lumber king Simon Benson, who was Oregon's first promoter of tourism. He helped construct the Columbia Gorge Scenic Highway, which was completed in 1920, and then built a luxurious forty-two-room hotel on a cliff above the river. Known as the "Waldorf of the West" in its heyday, the resort attracted a clientele of wealthy easterners mingled with Hollywood celebrities Valentino, Clara Bow, and ... are reputed to have been guests. Over the years the hotel's glitter faded and eventually it became a retirement home. Recently, however, this inn was restored to the opulence of the roaring twenties. Today in the massive dining room overlooking the river, visitors can enjoy many of the dishes introduced here fifty years ago by the hotel's first manager and chef, Henry Thiele. His recipes have been preserved, and the most popular of them all is the poached fresh Columbia River salmon.

## SPLIT PEA SOUP

This soup keeps very well under refrigeration and may easily be frozen.

*Serves sixteen as first course, eight as main course*
One 2- to 3-pound ham bone with some
   ham left on
2 bay leaves
2-1/2 to 3 quarts stock or water, to cover
1-1/2 pounds (approximately 3-1/4 cups)
   dried green split peas
1 onion, cut in medium dice
2 celery stalks, cut in medium dice
2 carrots, cut in small dice
1/2 to 1 teaspoon crumbled dried basil
1/4 teaspoon crumbled dried sage
Salt and freshly ground pepper to taste

Place bone and bay leaves in a large kettle and add stock to cover. Cover, bring to a boil, lower heat and cook slowly 2 hours. Add split peas and boil gently 2-1/2 to 3 hours. Add vegetables, herbs, salt, and pepper. Cook 30 minutes or until vegetables are just tender. Remove ham bone and, if desired, dice meat and return to soup.

## FRESH POACHED SALMON WITH SOUR CREAM DILL SAUCE

*Serves seven*

POACHING BROTH
1 quart water
1 small onion, finely diced
1 celery stalk, finely diced
1/2 teaspoon salt
2 whole cloves
1/2 lemon, thinly sliced

Seven 10-ounce salmon fillets
Dill Sauce, following

In a large flat pan, combine poaching broth ingredients. Cover, bring to a boil, lower heat, and boil gently 50 minutes.
   When ready to prepare fillets, place in poaching broth, adding water if needed to cover fillets completely. Bring to a *gentle* boil and cook slowly, at barely a simmer, for 15 to 20 minutes or until fish flakes easily with a fork. Remove with a slotted spoon, place on heated plates, and glaze with Dill Sauce.

DILL SAUCE
2-1/2 cups mayonnaise
1 cup sour cream
3 tablespoons freshly grated Parmesan
  cheese
3 tablespoons minced fresh dill
3 tablespoons finely minced onion
2 garlic cloves, finely minced
1-1/2 tablespoons cider vinegar
2 teaspoons freshly ground pepper
2 teaspoons fresh lemon juice
2 teaspoons Worcestershire sauce

In a mixing bowl, combine all ingredients
thoroughly.

## CHOCOLATE MOUSSE

*Serves eight to ten*
6 eggs, separated
1/2 cup Kahlúa
3 tablespoons unsweetened cocoa
1/2 cup honey
1 cup heavy cream
2 tablespoons Kahlúa
2 squares (2 ounces) semisweet chocolate,
  cut up
Grated semisweet chocolate

Put egg yolks in a ble
1/2 cup Kahlúa, unsw
honey. Blend until smooth.
heavy saucepan and, stirring con
bring to a slow boil. Cook and stir un
thick and syrupy. Remove from heat and
purée in blender again. Transfer to a
bowl and refrigerate until cool. Whip egg
whites until stiff and fold in cooled
chocolate mixture. In a blender container,
put 1/4 cup of cream, 2 tablespoons
Kahlúa, and cut-up chocolate. Blend;
mixture does not have to be smooth.
Combine with egg mixture. Whip remaining cream into stiff peaks and fold
chocolate mixture in. Transfer to serving
bowl, cover with plastic wrap, and refrigerate. When ready to serve, top with
grated chocolate.

NOTE: If you intend to hold mousse
more than one day, soften 1 tablespoon
unflavored gelatin in a little water and
add to blender with egg yolks.

# The Captain Whidbey
## Coupeville, Washington

Sir George Vancouver discovered Whidbey Island during his explorations of Puget Sound in the 1790s and named it after one of his captains. In 1904 Judge Lester Carlos Still built a rustic resort of logs above a pretty cove on this long, narrow island. After surviving usage as a girls' school, a post office, and a general store during the 1920s, the Captain Whidbey has operated continuously as an inn—for the past twenty years under the ownership of the Stone family. The dining room, with its two fireplaces, offers a magnificent view of Mount Baker across the cove, and a menu that features the superb seafood of the area. When salmon is in season, the following is one of the most popular dishes.

## SALMON DIJON

*Serves four*
Four 8-ounce salmon fillets
Unbleached flour
Safflower or corn oil for pan-frying
3 tablespoons sour cream
1 tablespoon Dijon-style mustard

Preheat oven to 400°F. Dredge salmon fillets in flour and fry in hot oil until almost tender. Transfer to baking dish. Combine sour cream and mustard. Spread over fillets and bake 3 minutes or until bubbly and starting to turn golden.

## WHIDBEY TRIFLE

Make your own pound cake (page 153), or purchase your favorite for this unusual trifle. Packaged or homemade vanilla pudding may be used.

*Makes one trifle serving ten to twelve*
1 pound cake
2/3 cup sherry
2/3 cup strawberry jam
2 cups vanilla pudding
1-1/2 cups sour cream
Toasted sliced almonds
1/2 cup heavy cream, whipped with
Grated nutmeg to taste

Cut cake 3/4 inch thick and layer half in bottom of a 2-quart glass bowl with straight sides. Sprinkle 1/3 cup of sherry over, spread evenly with 1/3 cup of jam, then 1 cup of pudding. Carefully spread with half of sour cream. Repeat layers, decorate with sliced almonds, and serve with whipped cream.

# The Shelburne Inn
*Seaview, Washington*

Seaview is the gateway to Washington's Long Beach Peninsula, the finger of land that separates Willapa Bay from the Pacific Ocean. At the turn of the century this was a popular vacation area, but of the many hotels of that period, the Shelburne—an 1896 Victorian—is all that remains. Originally built as a residence, a decade later it was joined to a similar building to become the Shelburne Hotel. Then after years of neglect, it was reopened in the 1970s as the Shelburne Inn by David Campiche and his wife Laurie Anderson. The hotel's restaurant is independently operated and has a reputation as one of southwestern Washington's finest eating places. Recently, new owners took over the restaurant operation and put chef Lorren Garlichs in charge. The following recipes reflect his pride in utilizing the natural bounty of the area: mussels picked at low tide from rocky outcroppings in the Pacific; oysters from Willapa Bay, one of the great natural oyster beds of the world; Columbia River sturgeon, a giant armor-plated fish that can grow to forty feet in length and live to one hundred years; and cranberries from the reddish-purple vines found abundantly in the bogs of the Long Beach Peninsula.

## INNKEEPER'S MUSSEL CHOWDER

*Serves four to six*

STEAMING LIQUID
1/4 pound butter
1/2 onion, sliced
1/2 large celery stalk, sliced
3 parsley stems
2 cups dry white wine

3 pounds mussels, well scrubbed
6 tablespoons butter
1 celery stalk, minced
2 onions, minced
1/2 bunch parsley, minced
1-1/2 pounds baking potatoes, peeled
   and cubed
1 tablespoon minced fresh basil
2-2/3 cups tomato purée
2 cups heavy cream
Salt and freshly ground pepper to taste

Place ingredients for steaming liquid in a steamer; add mussels. Cover, bring to a boil, and steam 5 to 10 minutes just until mussels open. Remove mussels. Strain steaming liquid and set aside. Remove meat from mussel shells, pulling out and discarding beard. Halve or quarter meat and set aside.

In a soup kettle, melt butter. Cover and cook celery, onions, and parsley until onions are translucent. Add potatoes and basil, cover, and cook over low heat until potatoes start to soften and are about three-fourths done. Add steaming liquid, tomato purée, and cream. Stirring to combine well, heat but do not boil. Season with salt and pepper, add mussels, reheat, and serve immediately.

## WILLAPA OYSTERS IN CHAMPAGNE SAUCE

*Serves one to two*
6 fresh oysters in shells
Rock salt
1/2 cup champagne
1 egg yolk
2 tablespoons Crème Fraîche, following

Shuck oysters, reserving half of shells, and pour oyster liquor into a small saucepan. Place oyster shells on a bed of rock salt in a shallow baking pan. Warm pan in oven. Place oysters and champagne in saucepan with liquor. Bring to a boil and reduce to two-thirds. Remove from heat and place oysters in shells. Keep warm. Beat egg yolk and gradually whisk in Crème Fraîche. Put over low heat and whisk until creamy. *Do not overheat.* Pour sauce over oysters and serve immediately.

CREME FRAÎCHE: Thoroughly combine equal parts sour cream and heavy cream. Let stand at room temperature overnight. Cover and refrigerate until ready to use.

## MATELOTE OF STURGEON

Sturgeon is a very meaty fish with an almost chickenlike taste. Since it is unavailable in many areas, a meaty white fish such as halibut may be substituted.

*Serves four*
Four 6-ounce fillets of sturgeon
2 tablespoons safflower or corn oil
1/2 onion, thinly sliced
1/4 pound fresh mushrooms, sliced
1/2 cup dry red wine
Lemon slices
Parsley sprigs

Preheat oven to 400°F. In a large ovenproof skillet, brown fillets in hot oil on both sides. Cover with onion and mushrooms and pour in wine. Bake 15 minutes or until fish flakes easily when prodded with a fork. Transfer fillets to serving plates and keep warm. Place skillet on high heat with wine, onions, and mushrooms. Reduce until thick enough to coat a spoon. Pour sauce over fish and serve garnished with lemon slices and parsley sprigs.

# CRANBERRY SHERBET

*Makes about two quarts*
4 cups fresh cranberries
4 cups water
2-1/4 cups granulated sugar
1 cup fresh orange juice
1 tablespoon freshly grated orange rind
2 egg whites
Whole cranberries
Fresh mint sprigs

In a large saucepan, cook cranberries in water until soft. Force through a sieve, discarding skins. Return to saucepan and stir in sugar, orange juice, and orange rind. Stirring to dissolve sugar, bring to a boil and cook 5 minutes. Cool. Beat egg whites until stiff but not dry. Gently fold in several cups of cranberry mixture, then fold into remaining cranberry mixture.

Place in an ice cream machine and follow manufacturer's directions for making sherbet. Or pour into a large shallow pan and freeze until slushy. Remove to a large bowl and beat. Return to pan and again freeze until slushy. Beat and pack into freezer containers. Freeze until sherbet consistency. Top each serving with a whole cranberry and a mint sprig.

# BREAD & BREAKFAST

*From the Atlantic to the Pacific*

# The Mainstay Inn
*Cape May, New Jersey*

In 1872 a pair of wealthy gamblers built a lavish Italianate villa at Cape May on the southernmost tip of New Jersey to use as an exclusive clubhouse where their friends could gamble in private. Extravagance was the byword in building and furnishing this Victorian mansion with its fourteen-foot ceilings, ornate plaster moldings, twelve-foot mirrors, and marble-topped sideboards. In 1976 Tom and Sue Carroll bought the former clubhouse for a bed and breakfast inn. The elegant nineteenth-century atmosphere and many of the original furnishings remain. There's no gambling today, except for a friendly game of cards in the parlor, but the Carrolls offer their guests many diversions of the Victorian era: croquet on the lawn, afternoon tea on the veranda, and ample breakfasts at the dining room's massive wooden table.

## GINGERY APPLE RINGS

*Serves four*
4 tablespoons butter
1/4 cup honey
1/2 teaspoon ground ginger
2 tablespoons fresh lemon juice
4 medium cooking apples, unpeeled

In a large skillet, melt butter. Blend in honey, ginger, and lemon juice. Cook 5 minutes, stirring occasionally. Wash, core, and slice apples into 1/2-inch rings. Turning occasionally, cook apple rings in honey-butter mixture 4 to 5 minutes. Serve warm or at room temperature.

## COMPANY EGGS

*Serves six to eight*
1/2 pound grated Swiss cheese
4 tablespoons butter
1 cup heavy cream
1/2 teaspoon salt
Dash freshly ground pepper
1/2 tablespoon dry mustard
12 eggs, lightly beaten
Minced fresh parsley or parsley sprigs

Preheat oven to 325°F. Spread cheese on bottom of buttered shallow baking dish. Dot with butter. Mix cream and seasonings. Pour half of cream over cheese. Add eggs and pour rest of cream on top. Bake 30 minutes or until cooked to taste. Garnish with parsley and serve with sausage and coffee cake.

## COFFEE CAKE EXCEPTIONALE

*Makes one large coffee cake*
3/4 cup butter at room temperature
1-1/2 cups granulated sugar
3 eggs
1/2 tablespoon pure vanilla extract
3 cups unbleached flour
1/2 tablespoon baking powder
1/2 tablespoon baking soda
1/4 teaspoon salt
1-1/2 cups sour cream

FILLING
1/2 cup firmly packed brown sugar
1/2 cup chopped pecans
1/2 tablespoon ground cinnamon

Preheat oven to 350°F. Butter and lightly flour a tube pan. In a mixing bowl, cream butter and sugar until light. One at a time beat in eggs, then vanilla. Combine dry ingredients and stir in alternately with sour cream.

Combine filling ingredients. Ladle half of batter into prepared pan. Sprinkle evenly with filling and spread remaining batter over. Bake 50 minutes or until cake pulls slightly away from sides of pan and a cake tester inserted in center comes out clean. Remove to a wire rack, cool slightly, and serve warm.

## PUMPKIN MUFFINS

*Makes one dozen*
1 egg
1/2 cup milk
1/2 cup pumpkin purée
4 tablespoons margarine, melted
1-1/2 cups unbleached flour
1/2 cup sugar
2 teaspoons baking powder
1/2 teaspoon salt
1/2 teaspoon ground cinnamon
1/2 teaspoon grated nutmeg
1/2 cup raisins

Preheat oven to 400°F. In a large bowl, beat egg lightly and blend in milk, pumpkin purée, and margarine. In a sifter, measure flour, sugar, baking powder, salt, and spices. Sift into pumpkin purée mixture; blend *just* until ingredients are moistened. Fold in raisins and spoon into well-buttered muffin tins. Bake 15 minutes or until a cake tester inserted in center comes out clean. Serve with honey or apple butter.

# Beaumont Inn
### Harrodsburg, Kentucky

Located in Kentucky's famous Blue Grass region, the columned antebellum structure that now houses the Beaumont Inn was built in 1845 for a girl's college known as the Greenville Female Institute. It was later renamed Daughter College and finally Beaumont College. In 1917 Glave and Annie Goddard purchased the college buildings and the surrounding thirty acres for the Beaumont Inn; Mrs. Goddard was a graduate of Daughter College and a former teacher at Beaumont College. The inn has been owned and operated

since by Goddard descendants, with great-grandson Chuck Dedman now serving as manager. The typical Kentucky-style cooking is done by family members from recipes passed down from generation to generation.

## CORNMEAL MUFFINS

*Makes one dozen*
1 egg, lightly beaten
1-1/2 cups buttermilk
2 cups yellow cornmeal
1 teaspoon baking soda
1 teaspoon salt

Preheat oven to 450°F. Grease 12 muffin tins and heat. In a large bowl, combine egg and buttermilk. Combine cornmeal, baking soda, and salt. Stir into milk mixture and spoon into muffin tins. Bake 10 minutes or until muffins shrink slightly from sides of tins and a cake tester inserted in center comes out clean. Serve immediately.

## BUTTERMILK BISCUITS

*Makes about one dozen*
2 cups unbleached flour
1 teaspoon baking powder
1/2 teaspoon baking soda
1/2 teaspoon granulated sugar
1/2 teaspoon salt
1 tablespoon plus 1 teaspoon lard or
  shortening, chilled
1 cup buttermilk

Preheat oven to 450°F. In a mixing bowl, thoroughly combine flour, baking powder, soda, sugar, and salt. Crumble in lard with fingers, and with a fork mix in buttermilk just until moistened. Gently form into a ball and transfer to a lightly floured board. Pat and roll approximately 3/4 inch thick. Cut with a 2-inch cutter and transfer to a lightly greased baking sheet. Bake 8 to 10 minutes until golden. Serve immediately.

# Cottage Plantation
### *St. Francisville, Louisiana*

Judge Thomas Butler built the Cottage Plantation in 1795 and hosted many famous people over the years, including Andrew Jackson, who stayed there after the Battle of New Orleans. Set on 360 verdant acres of dogwood, mimosa, camellias, and live oaks dripping with Spanish moss, the Cottage has been an inn since 1952. It is one of the few remaining antebellum plantations with all outbuildings intact: schoolhouse, outside kitchen, barns, milk house and slave quarters. The house's furnishings include many of the original antiques. The formal dining room, appointed with bone china and silver, is the setting for hearty Southern breakfasts: eggs, bacon, grits, and biscuits.

## ESTELLE'S BISCUITS

These light and flaky biscuits are quite sweet; adjust sugar measurement according to taste.

*Makes fifteen*
2-1/2 cups unbleached flour
1/2 tablespoon baking powder
1/2 teaspoon salt
3 tablespoons granulated sugar
3/4 cup shortening or lard
About 2/3 cup milk

Preheat oven to 450°F. Combine flour, baking powder, salt, and sugar. Cut in shortening until mixture is consistency of coarse cornmeal. With fork, stir in milk to moisten just until dough can be formed with fingers into a ball. Transfer to a lightly floured pastry board and knead gently 3 or 4 times. Pat and roll 3/4 inch thick. With a 2-inch cutter, cut into rounds. Place rounds on an ungreased cookie sheet and bake 10 minutes or until golden brown. Serve immediately.

# Deep Creek Lodge
*Bonners Ferry, Idaho*

The northern Idaho panhandle is a land of sky-blue lakes and forested mountains, a mecca for hunters and fishermen. Since the 1930s travelers through the area have found food and refreshment at a roadhouse near the banks of Deep Creek, and later as cabins were added they found overnight accommodations. Today Deep Creek Lodge, presently owned by Jean and Larry Welch, is one of the more popular resorts in North Idaho. The food is simple country western; Alaska Gold, a hearty breakfast dish, is the house specialty.

## ALASKA GOLD

*Serves two to three*
1 large baking potato (10 to 12 ounces)
1/2 cup finely chopped onions
Salt and freshly ground pepper to taste
Bacon drippings for pan-frying
1/3 to 1/2 cup grated Cheddar cheese
Eggs and toast of choice

Peel potato, halve, cover with water, and boil *just* until potato starts to soften. Drain and cool. Grate coarsely and toss with onions, salt, and pepper. Heat bacon drippings and turn potato mixture into a skillet, forming a loose cake with a spatula and pressing down gently. Cook until nicely browned on bottom. Adding more bacon drippings if needed, flip cake over and brown other side. Sprinkle cheese over, cover, and cook until cheese is melted. Serve immediately with eggs and toast.

# The Hope Houses
## Geyserville, California

Until recently, the northern part of California's Sonoma County, through which the Russian River winds its way into the Pacific, was mostly farmlands and orchards. Vineyards were scattered about, but most of the grapes were destined for jug wines. In the 1970s, however, vintners found the Russian River Valley capable of producing premium bottlings, and the area now competes with neighboring Napa Valley as a major wine center. Inevitably, country inns have sprung up to house those who come to taste the wines. One of the newest of these inns occupies two of the valley's oldest quarters—a century-old Italianate Victorian and a 1904 Queen Anne cottage—in the tiny town of Geyserville. Bob and Rosalie Hope faithfully restored the buildings, linked their name to the original owners' names, and rechristened the inns Hope-Bosworth House and Hope-Merrill House. Breakfasts here are centered around Rosalie Hope's homemade breads and preserves.

FRUIT BUTTER

*Makes about 1-1/2 cups*
1/4 pound butter at room temperature
4 ounces cream cheese at room temperature
1/2 cup lightly crushed fresh fruit such as strawberries, raspberries, peaches

Cream butter and cheese thoroughly and blend in fruit. Pack into individual ramekins and chill. Serve with Strawberry Bread or other muffins and breads.

## STRAWBERRY BREAD

A moist bread that may serve as a dessert topped with whipped cream and whole strawberries.

*Makes one loaf*
1-1/2 cups unbleached flour
1 cup granulated sugar
1/2 tablespoon ground cinnamon
1/2 teaspoon baking soda
2 eggs
2/3 cup safflower or corn oil
One 12-ounce basket strawberries, sliced
2/3 cup chopped pecans
Fruit Butter, page 141

Preheat oven to 350°F. Sift flour, sugar, cinnamon, and baking soda. In a large bowl, beat eggs lightly and blend in oil. Add flour mixture and stir to blend *just* until dry ingredients are moistened. Gently fold in strawberries and pecans; do not overmix. Pour into buttered and lightly floured 8-1/2x4-1/2x2-1/2-inch loaf pan. Bake 1 hour and 5 minutes or until bread pulls away from sides of pan and cake tester inserted in center comes out clean. Remove to cooling rack and let stand 10 minutes. Turn out onto rack, turn right side up, and cool. Slice thinly and serve with Fruit Butter.

# Little River Inn
## Little River, California

The Little River Inn, just south of Mendocino, is probably the oldest continuously operated inn on California's north coast. The inn's main building was built in 1853 as a residence by lumber and shipping tycoon Silas Coombs, a transplanted New Englander like most of the area's other early settlers. In 1929, with the demise of the once-prosperous logging industry, the Coombs family took in paying guests and eventually expanded Little River into an inn of fifty rooms with the addition of annexes and nearby cottages. Today the inn is still owned by Coomb's descendants, and meals are served in the main house. For years the stellar attraction here was abalone picked from the rocks of Little River Cove below. Due to its price and irregular availability, abalone doesn't often appear on the menu these days. But Little River Inn is almost as well known for its most popular breakfast item, Ole's Swedish Hotcakes.

## OLE'S SWEDISH HOTCAKES

*Serves four*

1 cup unbleached flour
1 teaspoon granulated sugar
1 teaspoon baking powder
1/4 teaspoon salt
1-1/2 cups milk
1/2 cup half-and-half cream
3 eggs, separated
6 tablespoons butter, melted and slightly
  cooled
Safflower or corn oil and/or butter for
  cooking

Mix dry ingredients thorough[ly] in milk and cream. Beat yolks into batter. Whip egg whites until stiff but not dry; fold into batter, stirring gently to incorporate whites. Batter will be slightly lumpy. Stir in melted and cooled butter. Brush griddle with oil and/or butter to lightly coat and heat to 425°F. Pour just under 1/4 cup of batter onto griddle for each hotcake. Hotcakes will spread to 3-1/2 to 4 inches in diameter. Cook until bubbles start to form on top, lift edge with spatula to make sure cake is browned, and flip over. Brown other side and serve at once.

# Old Monterey Inn
*Monterey, California*

In 1929 Carmel Martin, Sr., a former mayor of Monterey, built this stately Tudor mansion on an oak-studded hillside above the town. In 1968, Ann and Gene Swett bought the house and a decade later—after their six children were raised—turned it into an inn, one of the loveliest in the state. Breakfast is the only meal served here, but it's a memorable event whether partaken in bed, in the formal dining room cheered by a fire on cold mornings, or out in the beautiful gardens rampant with roses, hydrangeas, azaleas, and rhododendrons. The Swetts serve fresh orange juice afloat with sliced bananas, and an assortment of home-baked breakfast breads, two of which follow.

## BANANA MUFFINS

*Makes three dozen*
1 cup margarine
2 cups granulated sugar
6 very ripe bananas, gently mashed
   with a fork
4 eggs, well beaten
1-1/4 cups unbleached flour
1-1/4 cups whole-wheat pastry flour
1 teaspoon salt
2 teaspoons baking soda
1/4 to 1/2 cup any of the following, alone
   or in combination:
      oatmeal
      soy granules
      wheat germ
      sunflower seeds
      raisins
      chopped nuts
Poppy seeds, raisins, or chopped nuts

Preheat oven to 350°F. Cream margarine
and sugar. Stir in bananas and eggs until
well blended. Combine flours, salt, and
baking soda. Stir into banana mixture
just until dry ingredients are moistened.
Fold in oatmeal and/or other ingredients.
Ladle into 3 dozen paper-lined muffin
tins. Top with poppy seeds. Bake 20 to
30 minutes until lightly golden; muffins
should bounce back when
with fingers. Cool 2 minu
from tins. Cool on a cooli
freeze well.

## CHEESE ROLLS

*Makes seven rolls*
1 cup milk
4 tablespoons butter
1/4 teaspoon salt
Freshly ground white pepper to taste
1 cup unbleached flour
4 eggs
1/4 cup grated Cheddar cheese
1/2 cup grated extra-sharp Cheddar cheese

Preheat oven to 450°F. In a large
saucepan, combine milk, butter, salt, and
pepper. Slowly bring to a boil, stirring to
melt butter. All at once, add flour and
stir vigorously with a wooden spoon until
mixture is well mixed and forms a large
ball. Remove pan from heat. Two at a
time, beat in eggs, mixing and beating
well after each addition.
   Blend in Cheddar cheese. Drop 7 equal
spoonfuls onto a buttered cookie sheet
at least 2 inches apart. Sprinkle sharp
Cheddar cheese evenly over each roll.
Place in oven and immediately turn heat
down to 375°F. Bake 30 to 35 minutes
until golden and puffed. Serve at once
with unsalted butter and olallieberry or
other berry jam.

# San Ysidro Ranch
## *Montecito, California*

In 1786 the Spanish padres built their tenth California mission at Santa Barbara, surrounding it with cattle ranches and citrus groves that extended into the Santa Ynez Mountains which rise from the town. Part of this mountainside acreage is now the San Ysidro Ranch, a complex of stone and wooden cottages interspersed among gardens, orchards, and clusters of eucalyptuses and palms. When actor Ronald Colman owned the ranch in the thirties and forties, Sir Winston Churchill wrote part of his memoirs there; another guest, John Galsworthy, worked on the *Forsyte Saga* in one of the cottages. Laurence Olivier and Vivien Leigh were married in the gardens, and the John F. Kennedys chose San Ysidro for a honeymoon site. After years of neglect the ranch was purchased and revitalized in 1976 by New York hotelman Jim Lavenson and his wife Susie. Three meals a day are served in the former citrus-packing house, now an elegant restaurant. Breakfast is particularly pleasant, hearty enough to follow an early morning ride on one of the fine horses from the ranch's stable, yet sophisticated enough—like the following French toast recipe—to please the ranch's discriminating clientele.

## BRANDIED FRENCH TOAST WITH STRAWBERRY BUTTER

*Serves four*

2 eggs, beaten
1/4 to 1/2 cup half-and-half cream
1-1/2 to 2 tablespoons brandy
1/2 teaspoon ground cinnamon
1/2 teaspoon granulated sugar (optional)
8 to 10 slices slightly stale sweet French bread
Butter and safflower or corn oil for pan-frying
Powdered sugar
Strawberry Butter, following

In a large shallow dish, combine eggs, cream, brandy, cinnamon, and sugar. Soak bread slices in mixture about 10 minutes, turning once or twice, until liquid penetrates almost all the way through bread. Heat equal amounts butter and oil in skillet and pan-fry soaked bread slices until golden, turning once. Arrange slices on a serving plate and sprinkle with powdered sugar. Serve with Strawberry Butter.

STRAWBERRY BUTTER
1/4 pound unsalted butter at room
   temperature
2 tablespoons fresh strawberry purée
1-1/2 tablespoons honey
1/4 cup powdered sugar
Dash orange curaçao

Whip butter in mixing bowl of electric mixer until light and fluffy. Add remaining ingredients, beating until well blended. Spoon into a small crock or pipe into a small dish with a pastry bag fitted with a fluted tip.

NOTE: Strawberry Butter is also delicious on pancakes and croissants.

# Sutter Creek Inn
*Sutter Creek, California*

Jane Wey created the prototype for the California-style bed and breakfast hostelry. In 1966 she bought an 1859-vintage house in Sutter Creek, once a gold rush boomtown, in the Sierra Nevada foothills. After restoring the house, she went to work on the outbuildings—a woodshed, a carriage house, a storage shed, a laundry house—and turned them into striking guest accommodations decorated with flair in a colorful mishmash of styles and periods. Breakfast is served at long tables in the big country kitchen, with Jane often doing the cooking as she chats with guests and laces their coffee with brandy. Fresh fruit is served with a soufflé or corn bread or Jane's famous apple-nut pancakes.

## APPLE-NUT BUTTERMILK PANCAKES

*Serves twelve*
2-1/2 cups unbleached flour
2-1/2 teaspoons granulated sugar
1/2 tablespoon salt
2 teaspoons baking powder
1-1/4 teaspoons baking soda
3 eggs
2-1/2 cups buttermilk
2-1/2 tablespoons bacon drippings
1-1/2 cups firmly packed shredded tart
 apples
3/4 to 1-1/2 cups coarsely chopped
 walnuts, lightly dredged with flour

Combine flour, sugar, salt, baking powder, and baking soda. In a large bowl, beat eggs lightly and stir in buttermilk and bacon drippings. Add flour mixture and, with a wooden spoon, blend without beating until dry ingredients are moistened. Batter will be slightly lumpy. Stir in apples and nuts and let stand 30 minutes. Stirring lightly and frequently, ladle with a 1/4-cup measure onto a hot griddle and cook until small bubbles appear on surface. Lift edge with spatula to check browning and flip over to brown other side. Turn only once.

# COUNTRY KITCHEN
# B A S I C S

## BOUQUET GARNI

A *bouquet garni* is a small bundle of herbs, dried or fresh, tied together or tied in cheesecloth to make a small bag. It is used to season soups, stews, sauces. The classic mixture is available dried in specialty shops and most markets, and consists of the equivalent of 2 parsley sprigs, 1 small thyme sprig, and 1/2 bay leaf. Additions such as celery, garlic, oregano, tarragon, rosemary depend on the dish being cooked. Rosemary, for instance, complements lamb, tarragon complements chicken. Be cautious, however, for these herbs and some others have a distinct strong flavor that may overpower other flavors. Before serving, remove *bouquet garni*.

## CLARIFIED BUTTER

Melt butter over medium heat. Remove from heat and let stand to allow milk solids to settle. Spoon clear butter into a container and discard milk. Keep on hand in refrigerator.

## WHITE ROUX

Use equal amounts clarified butter and unbleached flour. In a heavy skillet, melt butter and stir in flour. Cook over medium heat, stirring constantly, 5 minutes. Do not allow to color. Cool and shape into tablespoon-sized balls. Wrap in foil and store in refrigerator.

## BROWN ROUX

Preheat oven to 300°F. Use equal amounts of clarified butter and unbleached flour. In an ovenproof skillet, melt butter and stir in flour. Place in oven and, stirring frequently, cook until light brown in color. Slow cooking is the secret, so be patient. The roux will have an aroma similar to toasted hazelnuts.

## COOKING HINTS

CARAMELIZE Heat granulated sugar in a heavy skillet, stirring constantly until sugar is liquified, brown, and caramel flavored.

DEGLAZE After cooking meats and poultry, let pan cool, remove fat with a spoon or paper towel, add liquid, and bring pan juices to a boil, scraping bottom and sides of pan. Cook and stir until reduced to desired consistency.

FLAMBÉ Heat liquor, pour into skillet over high heat, and ignite with a long match.

REDUCE Boil liquid until quantity is reduced to amount specified in recipe.

# PASTRY DOUGH

*Makes two 10-inch or three 9-inch pastry shells*
2-2/3 cups unbleached flour
1 to 1-1/2 teaspoons salt
1/4 pound butter, chilled and cut into bits
1/2 cup shortening or lard, chilled and
  cut into bits
Approximately 1/2 cup ice water

FOOD PROCESSOR METHOD With metal blade in place, put flour, salt, butter, and shortening in bowl of a processor. Process 8 seconds or until flour mixture is consistency of coarse cornmeal. With processor running, slowly pour ice water through tube, adding enough so that dough forms a loose ball. Do not add too much water or process too long or dough will toughen. Handling as gently and as little as possible, turn dough out onto a board and divide into 2 or 3 equal portions. Form each portion into a ball, place on waxed paper, and flatten into a disc about 3/4 inch thick. Wrap well and refrigerate at least 1 hour or overnight.

HAND METHOD In a large bowl, combine flour and salt. With fingers, pastry blender, or 2 forks, cut in butter and shortening to consistency of coarse cornmeal. Stirring with a fork, gradually add water until dough forms a loose ball. Proceed as above.

ROLLING THE DOUGH Remove 1 pastry disc from refrigerator and let stand at room temperature 4 to 5 minutes. Turn out onto lightly floured pastry board. Flatten with back of hand and flip over. Lightly flouring board and rolling pin, roll gently from center out. If dough appears to be sticking, carefully slip a spatula under it, lift up, lightly flour board, and flip over. Repeat until dough is desired size.

Place a pie pan upside down on dough and cut a circle 1-1/2 inches larger than pan. Place pan on counter and carefully lift pastry circle into pan. Gently press in and bring excess dough up onto rim of pan. Turn under and crimp edges. If using an unbaked pastry shell, wrap in foil and refrigerate.

PREBAKED PASTRY SHELL Prick bottom of shell with tines of a fork. Cut a circle of waxed paper or foil slightly larger than pan, fit it into shell, and chill at least 10 minutes. Preheat oven to 400°F. Fill shell with about 1-1/2 cups metal pie weights or raw rice. Bake 10 minutes. Remove weights and paper and return to oven for 5 or 10 minutes. Cool on a wire rack.

FULLY BAKED PASTRY SHELL After removing weights, reduce oven heat to 350°F. Bake 15 to 20 minutes or until golden. Cool on a wire rack.

EGG YOLK VARIATION Reduce water measurement by 1 tablespoon and add 1 egg yolk with flour and butter.

## POUND CAKE

*Makes one cake*
7 tablespoons butter, clarified (page 151)
1 teaspoon pure vanilla extract
6 eggs
1 cup granulated sugar
2 cups unbleached flour

Cool butter to lukewarm and stir in vanilla. Preheat oven to 350°F. In top of double boiler, beat eggs until lemon colored. Beat in sugar until fluffy. Over simmering water, beat with an electric mixer until smooth and thickened to consistency of softly whipped cream.
　　Remove pan from heat; cool *slightly*. Fold one third of flour into egg mixture. Fold remaining in quickly but gently. Scoop one fourth of this batter into a separate bowl and blend in butter mixture. Then fold into rest of batter. Pour into buttered and lightly floured 11x7x2-inch baking pan. Bake 45 minutes or until cake shrinks slightly away from sides of pan and cake tester inserted in center comes out clean. Cool on wire rack at least 15 minutes, turn out onto rack, and turn right side up.

## BAKING HINTS

MERINGUES AND EGG WHITES
• Take care not to overbeat egg whites. They should form stiff peaks, but not be dry.
• Add sugar to beaten egg whites very gradually and beat until mixture is glossy, but still forms peaks.
• When combining egg whites with batter, gently fold about one third of the batter into the beaten whites. Then gently fold this mixture into remaining batter.
• Meringues freeze beautifully.

OILING PANS With a pastry brush, generously spread pan with a mixture of 2 parts corn oil and 1 part liquid lecithin (available in health food stores). This is a foolproof method of preventing sticking.

SPLITTING A CAKE LAYER Insert 6 to 8 toothpicks at equal intervals around side of layer, midway between top and bottom of layer. Place a piece of thread on top of toothpicks on one side of layer and gradually pull it through cake, using rest of toothpicks as a guide.

# HINTS ON COOKING VEGETABLES

Most of the inns in this book serve fresh vegetables with their entrées, often from the inn's own garden. Most vegetables should be barely cooked until just tender. This preserves vitamins, minerals, flavor and texture. Vegetables may be cooked by the following general methods. For additional zest, add herbs and/or spices to cooking water. Save cooking or steaming water for stocks, sauces or other use.

## STEAMING

A collapsible perforated steaming rack that expands to fit any size saucepan is ideal for steaming vegetables. A colander, strainer or perforated tray may be substituted. Place rack in saucepan filled with 1 inch of water, place vegetables on rack, cover saucepan tightly and bring water to rapid boil. Lower heat, and keeping water at gentle boil, cook until vegetables are just tender.

*Recommended for Steaming* Artichokes, asparagus, beans, broccoli, cauliflower, carrots, kohlrabi, bok choy, Brussels sprouts, cabbage, corn on the cob, celery, peas, sunchokes, summer squash.

## BUTTER STEAMING

Melt butter in saucepan. Add vegetables and seasonings of choice. Cover and steam over medium heat until vegetables are just tender.

*Recommended for Butter Steaming* Brussels sprouts, shredded cabbage, carrots, celery, cucumbers, small whole onions, peas and snow peas, summer squash, sunchokes, spinach, celery root, tiny new potatoes.

## BRAISING

Sauté vegetables briefly in butter and/or oil. Cover with rich stock to half the depth of the vegetables, add seasonings of choice and bake or cook, covered, over medium-low heat until just tender.

*Recommended for Braising* Cabbage, celery, celery root, endive, lettuce, onions, sliced potatoes.

## BOILING

Boiling is the least recommended method for cooking vegetables because nutrients are lost in the cooking water. Very firm vegetables require this method. If boiling tender vegetables, boil in stock and reserve enriched stock for soups and sauces.

*Recommended for Boiling* Beets, potatoes, rutabagas, turnips, parsnips.

# Directory and Index of Inns

THE INN AT SAWMILL FARM
Route 100 and Crosstown Road
West Dover, VT 05356
Page 30

JAMIESON HOUSE
407 North Franklin
Poynette, WI 53955
Page 83

LITTLE RIVER INN
Little River, CA 95456
Page 142

THE LYME INN
Lyme, NH 03768
Page 27

MAGNOLIA HOTEL
6529 Yount Street
Yountville, CA 94599
Page 101

THE MAINSTAY INN
635 Columbia Avenue
Cape May, NJ 08204
Page 135

MALAGA INN
359 Church Street
Mobile, AL 36602
Page 47

MANKA'S/INVERNESS LODGE
Callender Way and Argyle
Inverness, CA 94937
Page 104

OLD LYME INN
85 Lyme Street
Old Lyme, CT 06371
Page 16

OLD MONTEREY INN
500 Martin Street
Monterey, CA 93940
Page 144

PELICAN INN
Muir Beach, CA 94965
Page 107

THE RED FOX TAVERN
2E Washington Street
Middleburg, VA 22117
Page 61

THE RED LION INN
Main Street
Stockbridge, MA 01262
Page 23

RIVER FOREST MANOR
600 East Main Street
Belhaven, NC 27810
Page 59

SAN BENITO HOUSE
Main Street
Route 1, Box 4A
Half Moon Bay, CA 94019
Page 110

SAN YSIDRO RANCH
900 San Ysidro Lane
Montecito, CA 93108
Page 146

SCHUMACHER'S
NEW PRAGUE HOTEL
212 West Main Street
New Prague, MN 56071
Page 75

THE SHELBURNE INN
Post Office Box 250
Seaview, WA 98644
Page 129

STONEHENGE
Route 7
Ridgefield, CT 06877
Page 19

SUTTER CREEK INN
75 Main Street
Sutter Creek, CA 95685
Page 147

UNION HOTEL
362 Bell Street
Post Office Box 616
Los Alamos, CA 93440
Page 116

VINEYARD HOUSE
Post Office Box 176
Coloma, CA 95613
Page 119

WAYSIDE INN
7783 Main Street
Middletown, VA 22645
Page 64

WOLF CREEK TAVERN
Post Office Box 97
Wolf Creek, OR 97497
Page 123

# Recipe Index

## Biographical Notes

CORALIE CASTLE is the author or co-author of seven cookbooks whose total print runs since 1972 have surpassed 400,000 copies. These include *The Art of Cooking for Two; Hors d'Oeuvre, Etc.; Real Bread;* and *Soup.* A native of Illinois, she presently lives in California's Marin County.

JACQUELINE KILLEEN is co-author of the guidebooks *Country Inns of the Far West* and *Best Restaurants San Francisco and Northern California.* She is also the author of a cookbook, *101 Secrets of California Chefs.* A native Californian, she presently lives in San Francisco.

This is the second book collaboration of Coralie Castle and Jacqueline Killeen. They were co-editors of *The Whole World Cookbook,* a collection of fifteen hundred recipes from 101 Productions' cookbooks, published in hardcover by Scribners in 1979.